Trace & Color

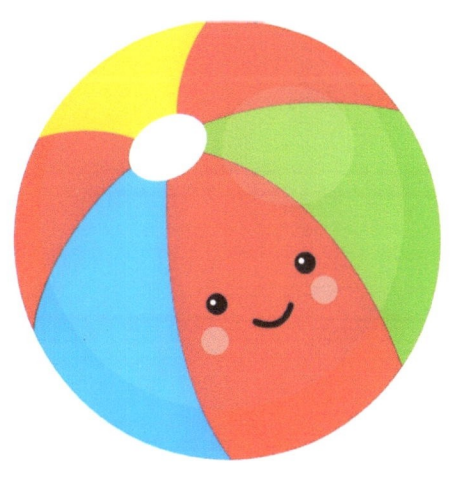

This book belongs to:

Band Aid

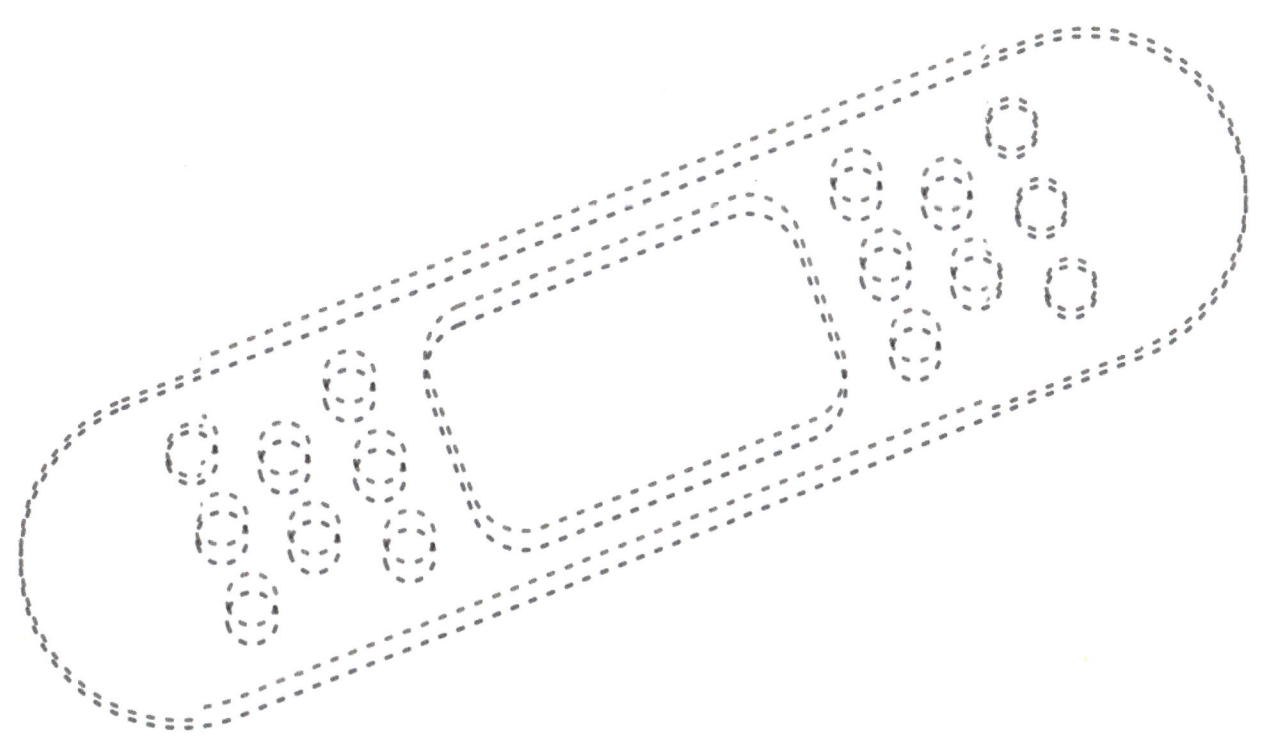

Beach Ball Beach Ball

Beach Ball Beach Ball

Beach Ball Beach Ball

Beach Ball Beach Ball

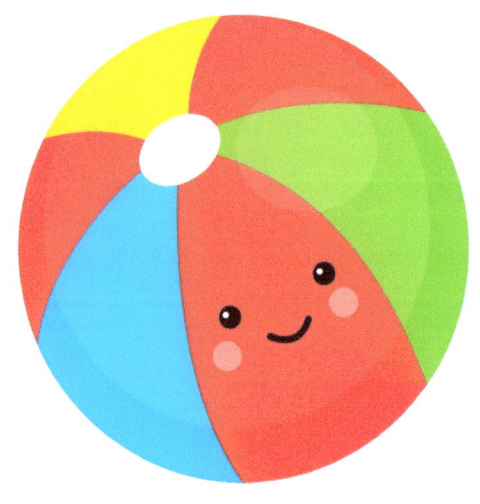

Beach Ball

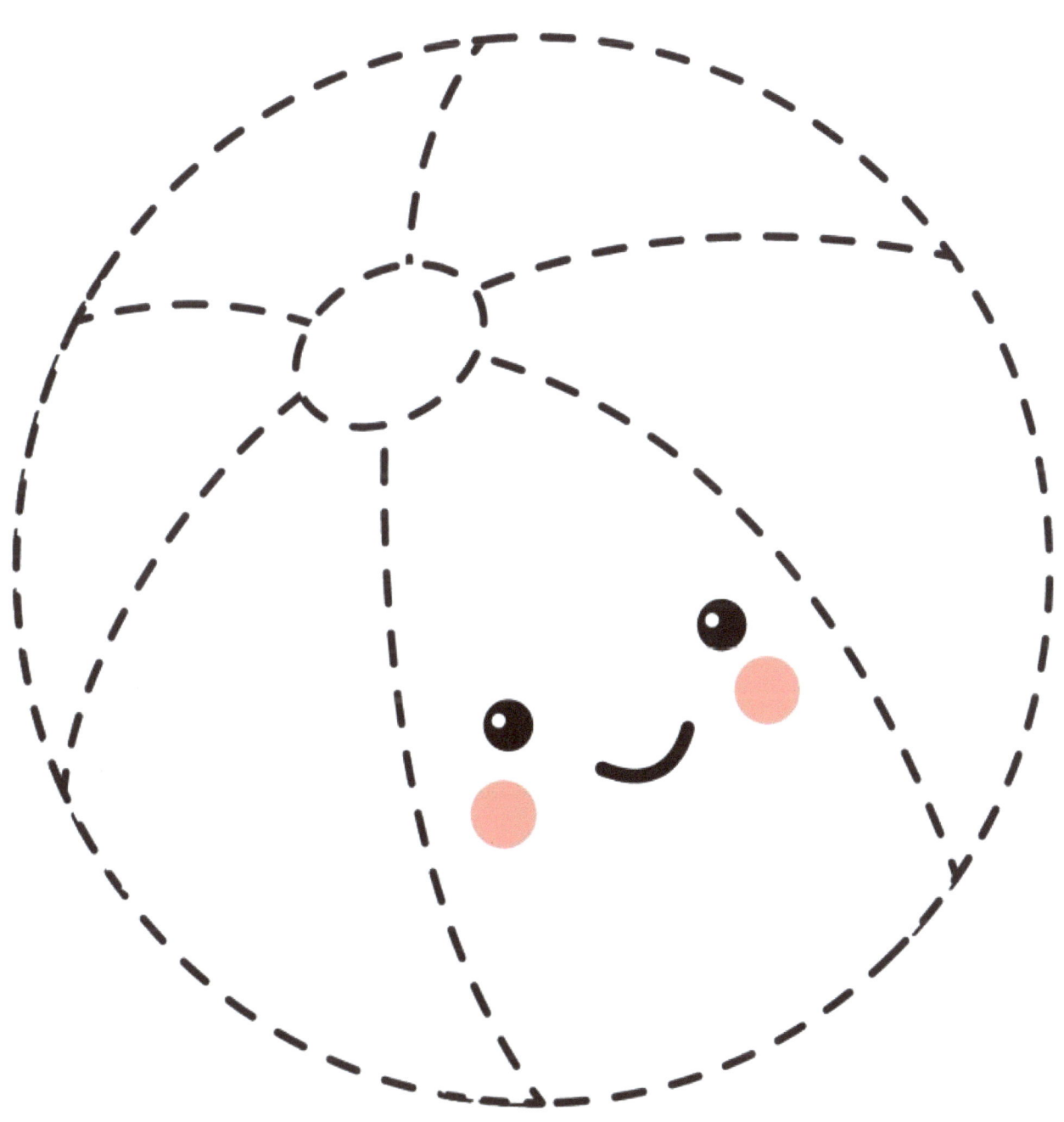

Bee Hive   Bee Hive

Bee Hive   Bee Hive

Bee Hive   Bee Hive

Bee Hive   Bee Hive

Beehive

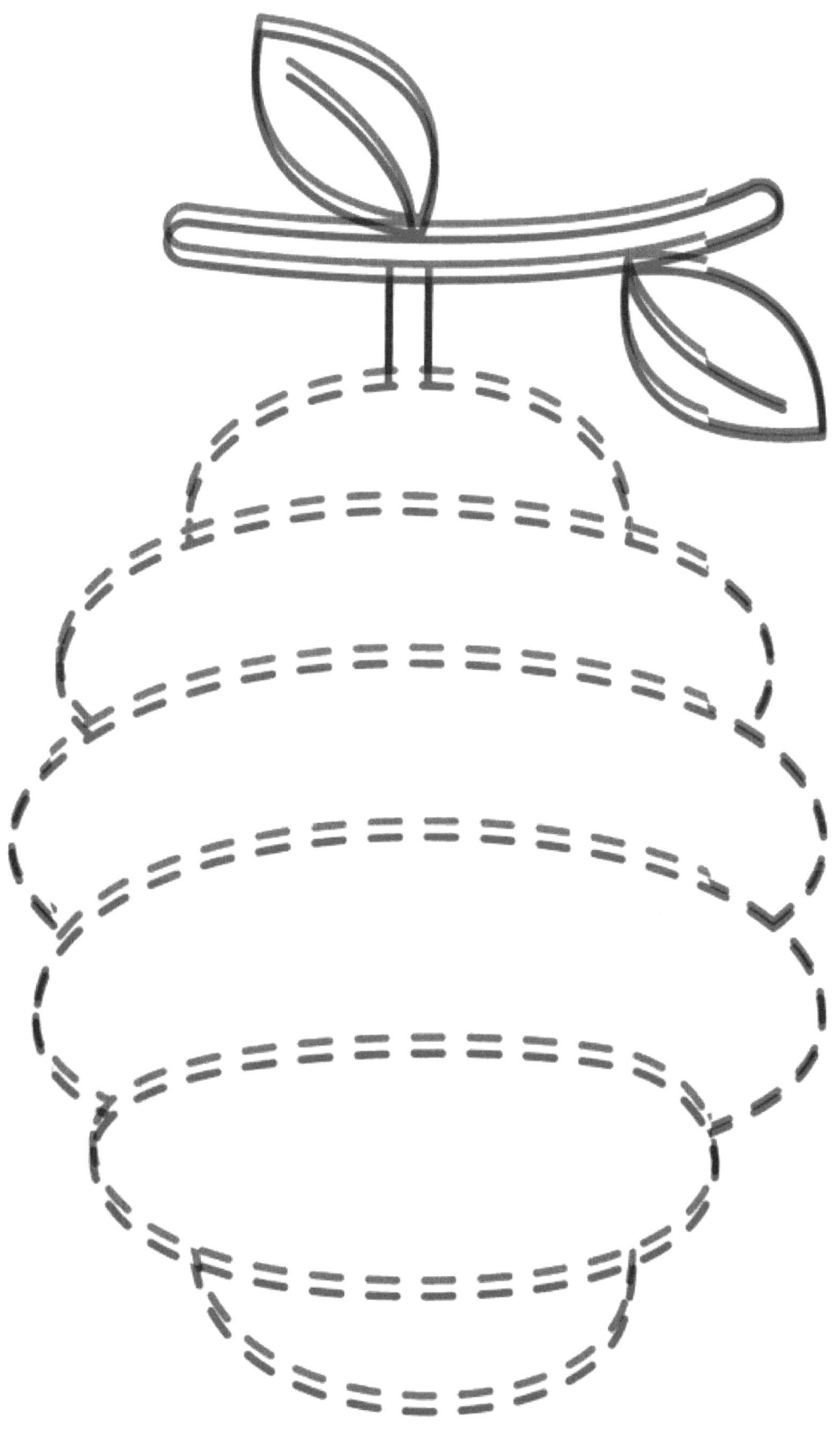

Blimp Blimp Blimp Blimp

Blimp Blimp Blimp Blimp

Blimp Blimp Blimp Blimp

Blimp Blimp Blimp Blimp

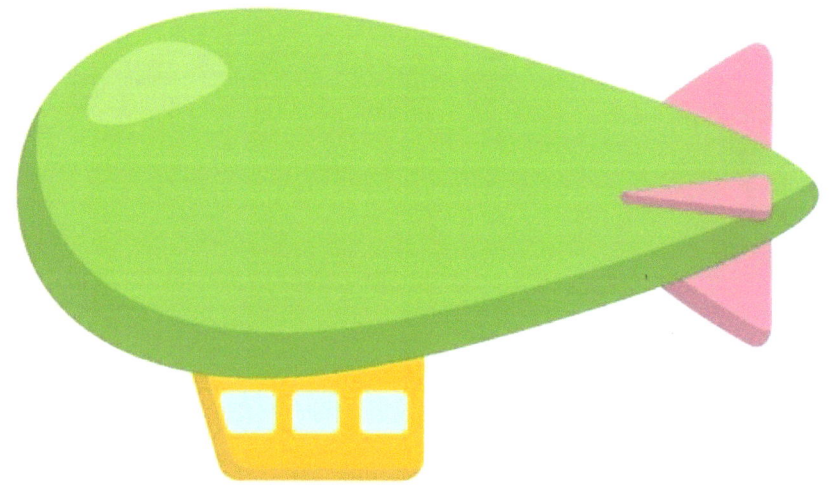

Blimp

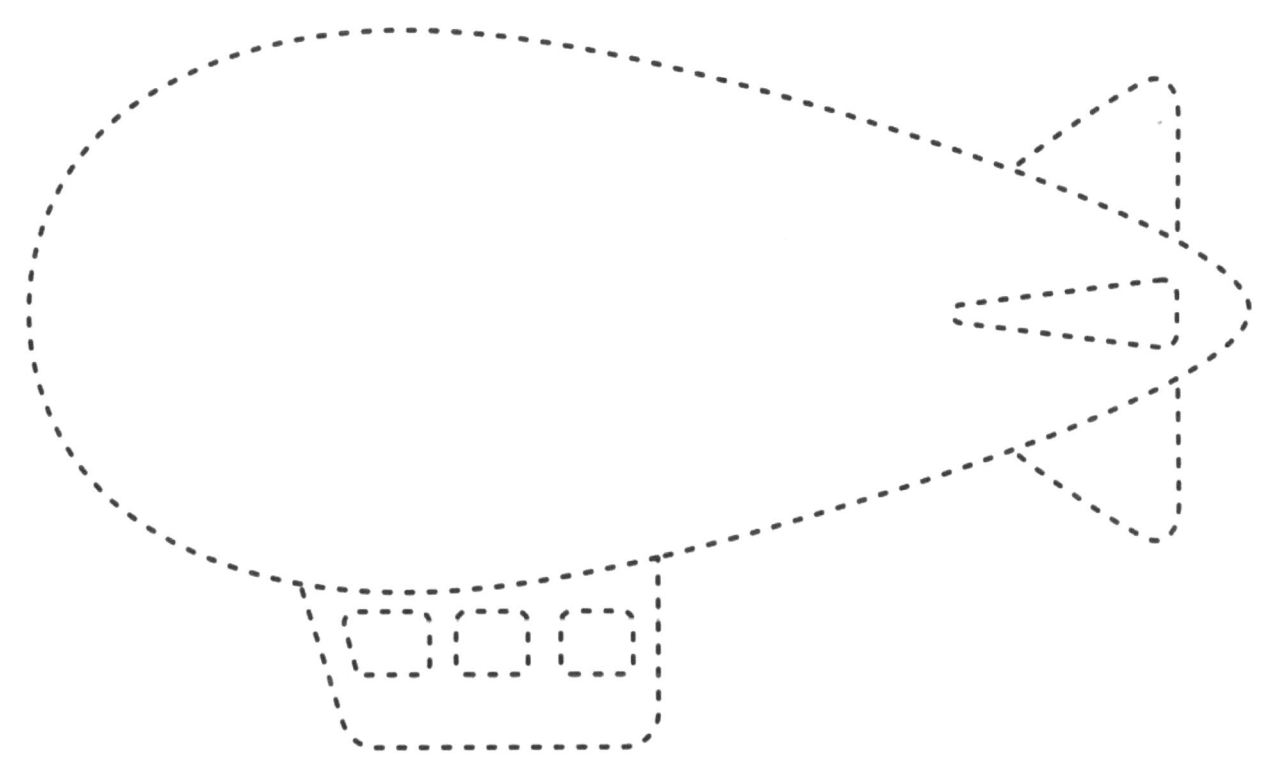

Bucket   Bucket   Bucket

Bucket   Bucket   Bucket

Bucket   Bucket   Bucket

Bucket   Bucket   Bucket

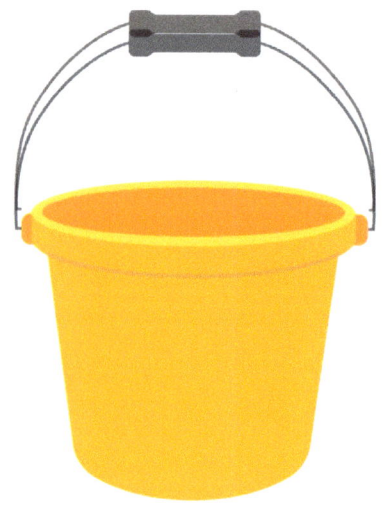

Bucket

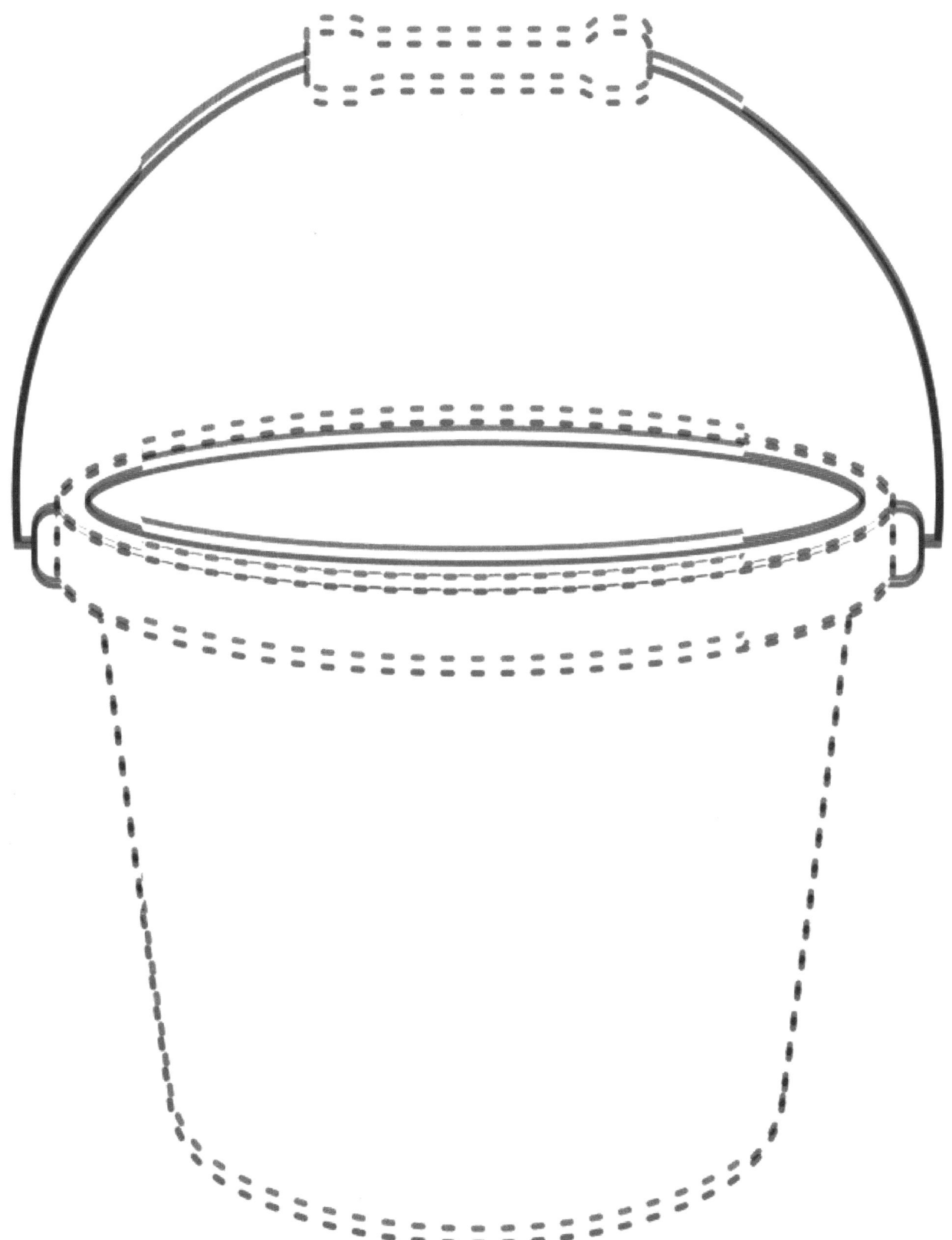

Chicken   Chicken
_____ _____

Chicken   Chicken
_____ _____

Chicken   Chicken
_____ _____

Chicken   Chicken
_____ _____

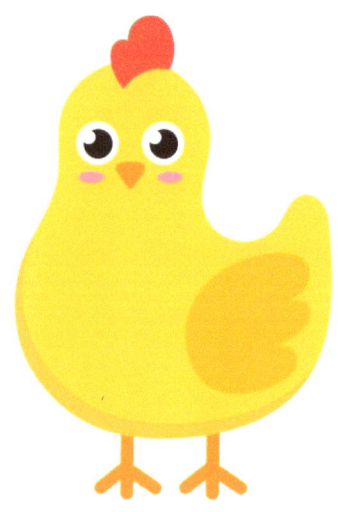

Chicken

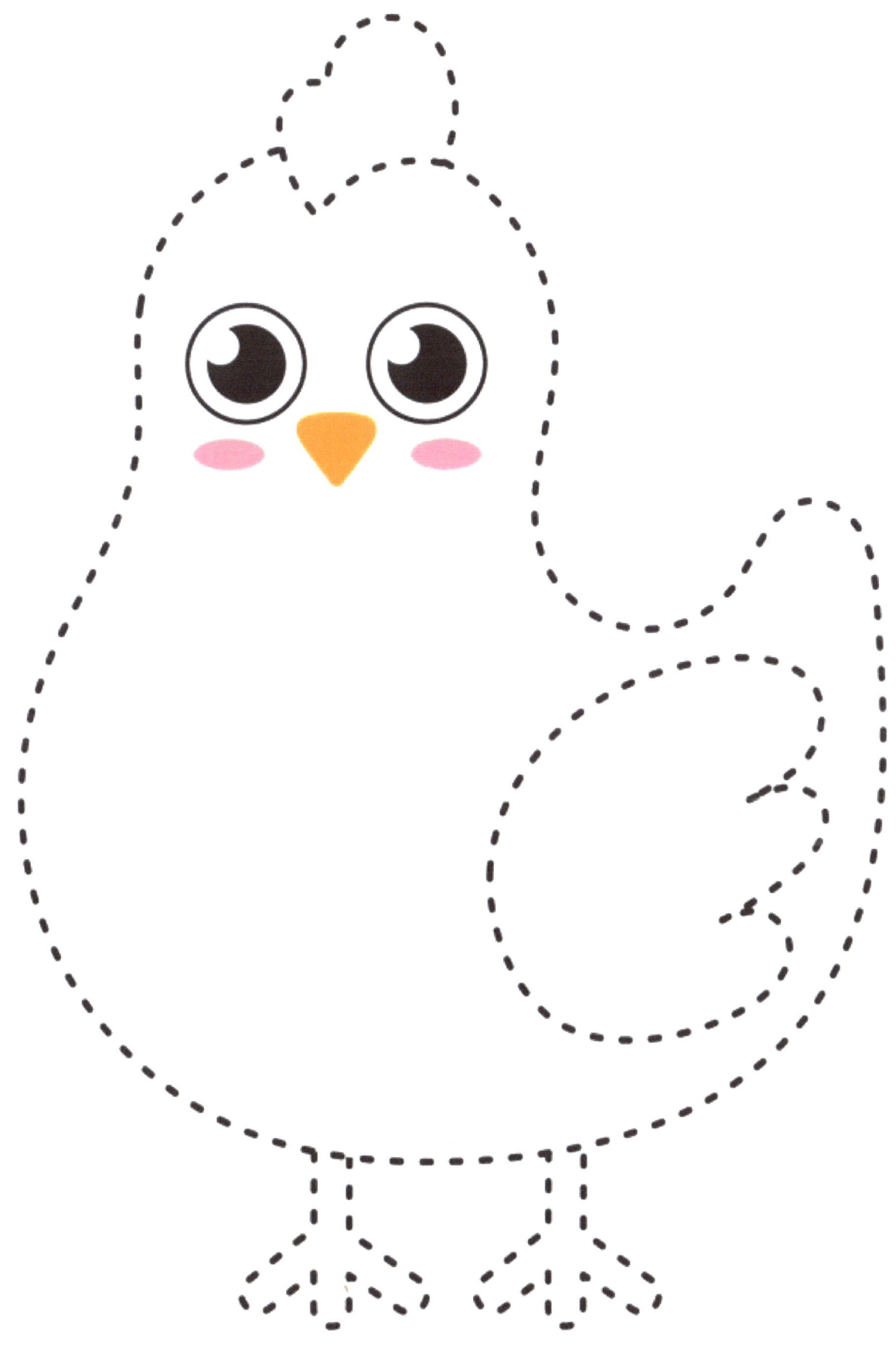

Doughnut   Doughnut

Doughnut   Doughnut

Doughnut   Doughnut

Doughnut   Doughnut

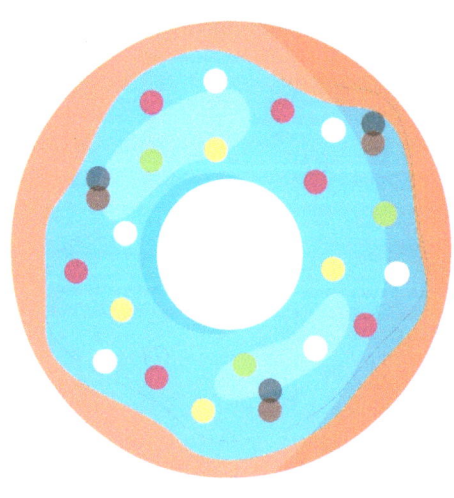

Doughnut

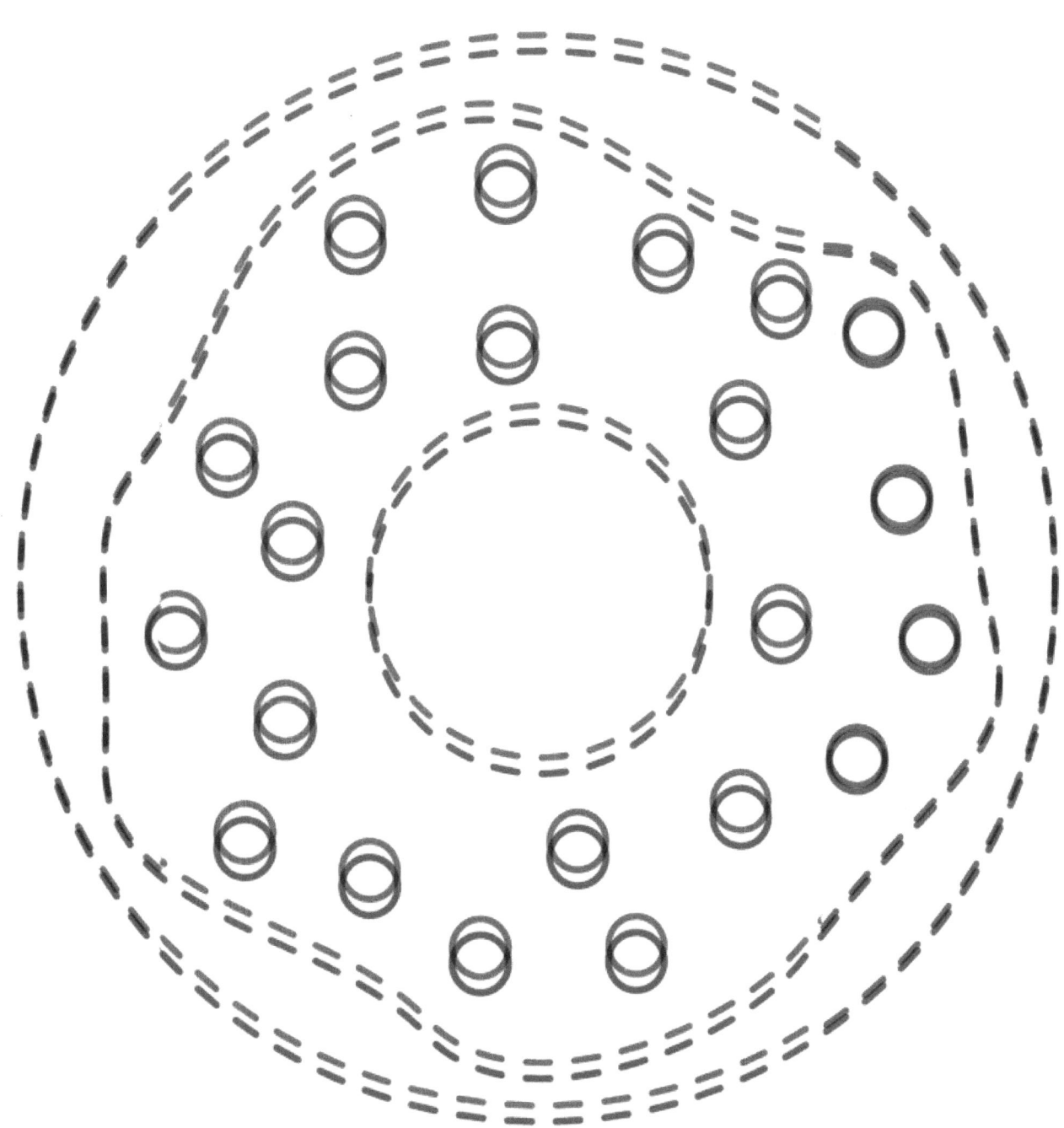

Dragon Fly   Dragon Fly

Dragon Fly   Dragon Fly

Dragon Fly   Dragon Fly

Dragon Fly   Dragon Fly

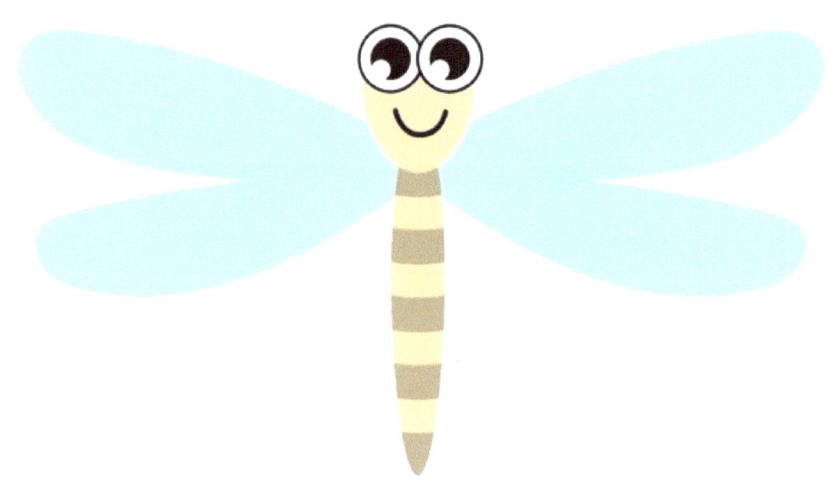

Dragonfly

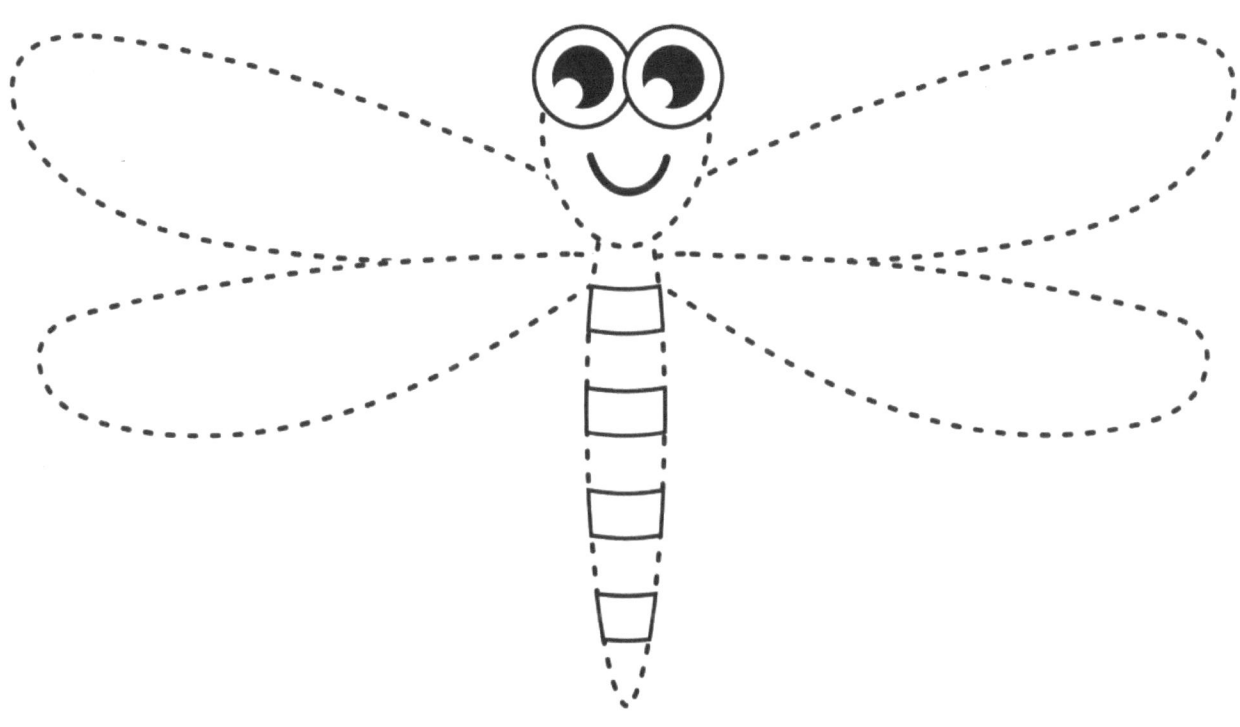

Electric Fan   Electric Fan

Electric Fan   Electric Fan

Electric Fan   Electric Fan

Electric Fan   Electric Fan

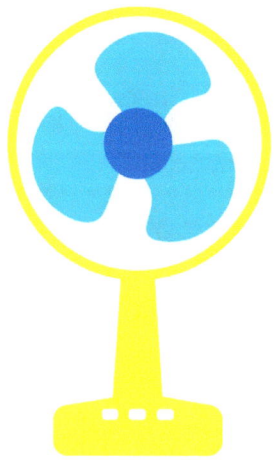

Electric Fan

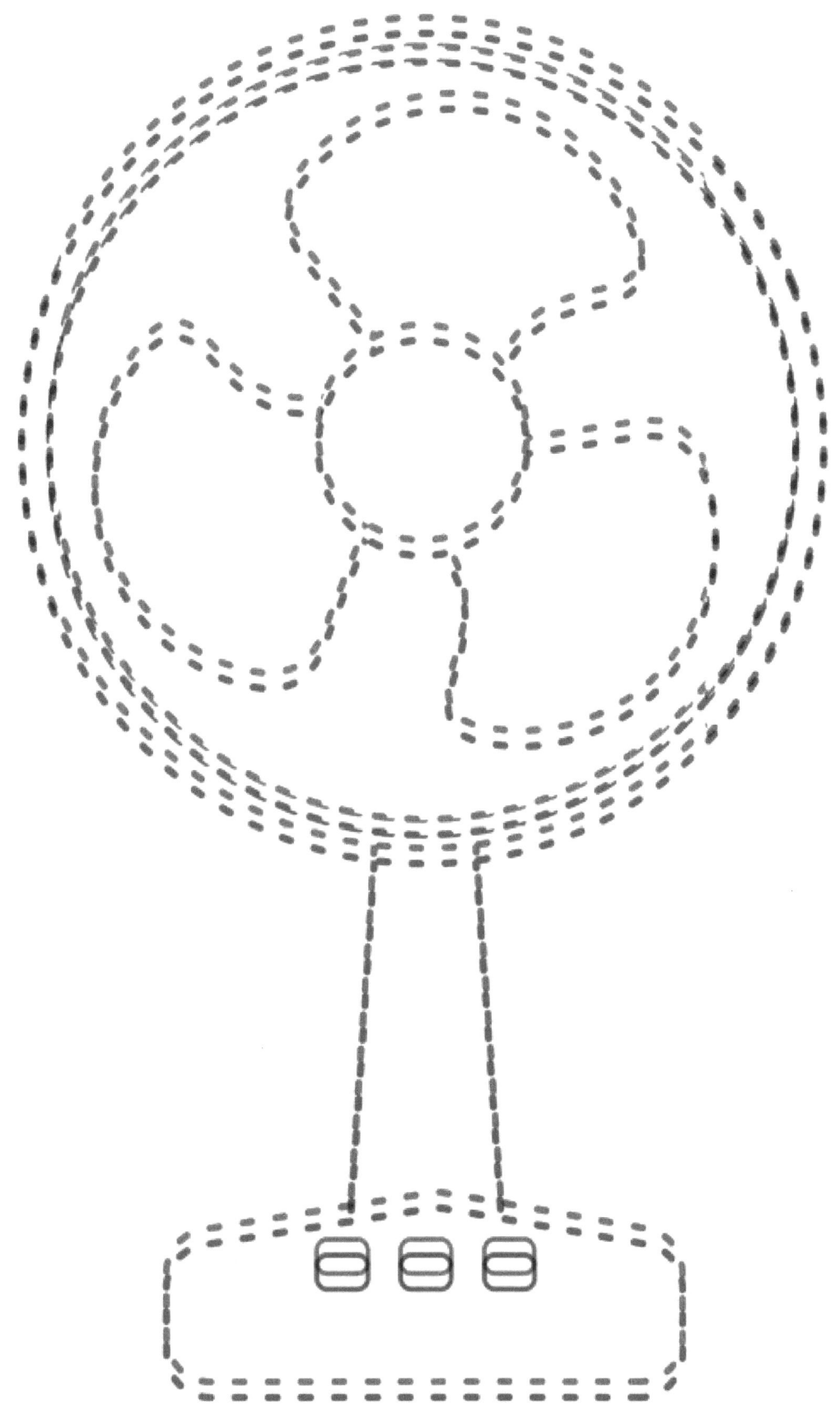

Fox   Fox   Fox   Fox

Fox   Fox   Fox   Fox

Fox   Fox   Fox   Fox

Fox   Fox   Fox   Fox

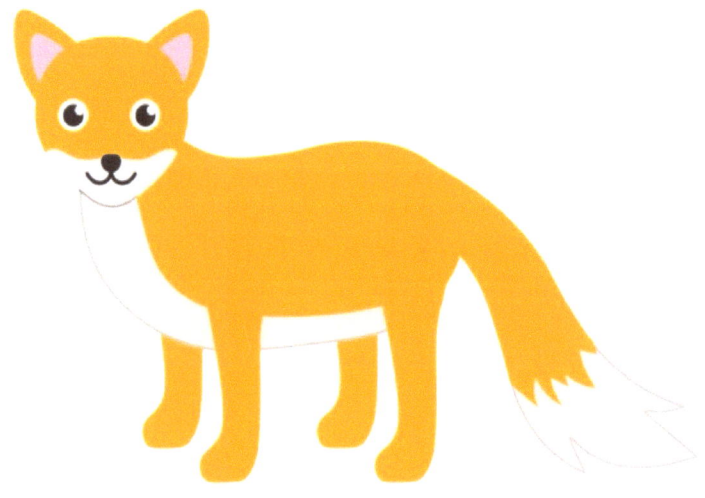

Fox

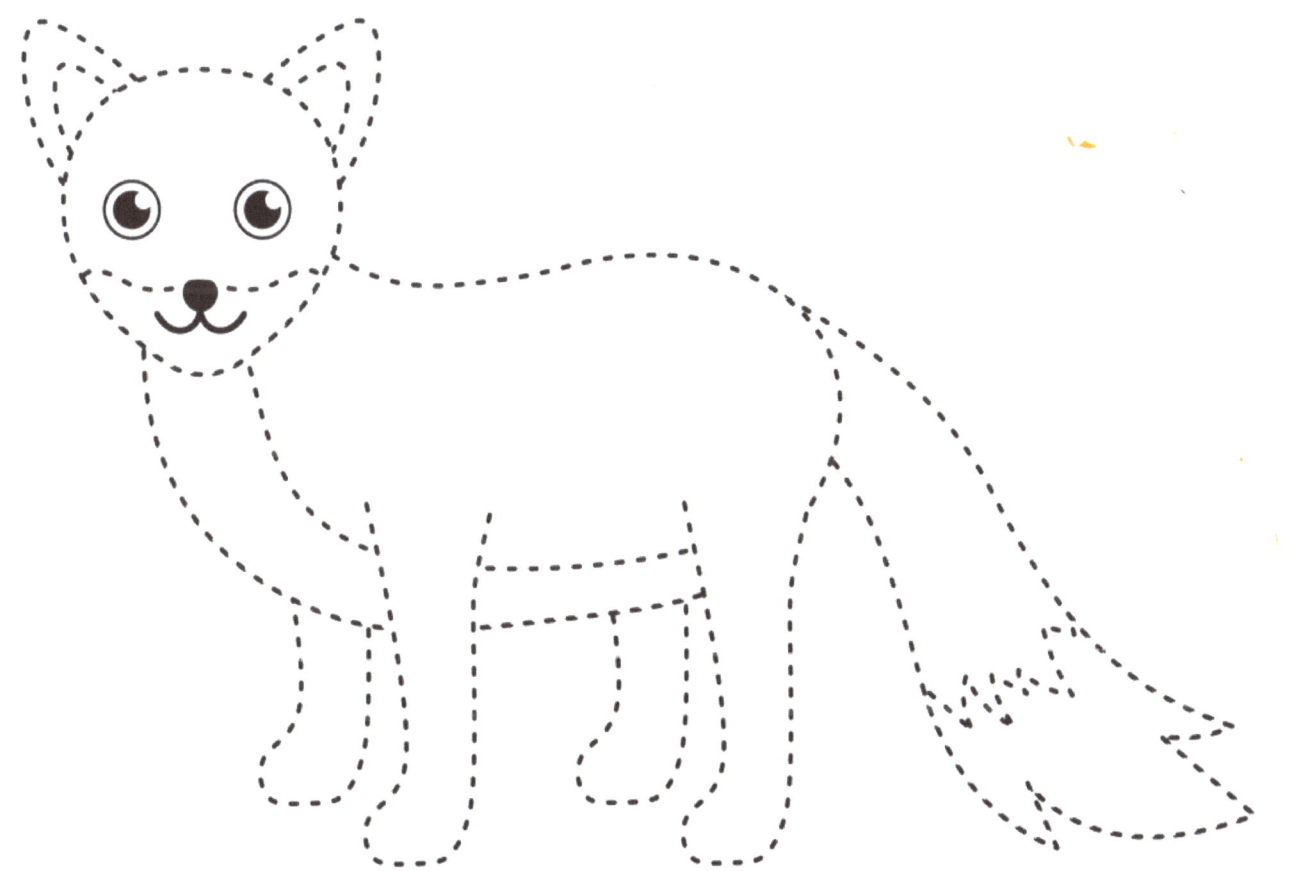

Frog   Frog   Frog   Frog

Frog   Frog   Frog   Frog

Frog   Frog   Frog   Frog

Frog   Frog   Frog   Frog

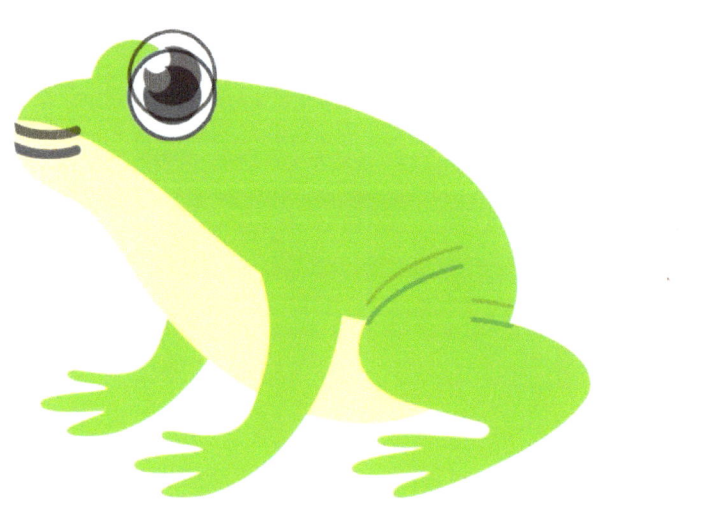

Frog

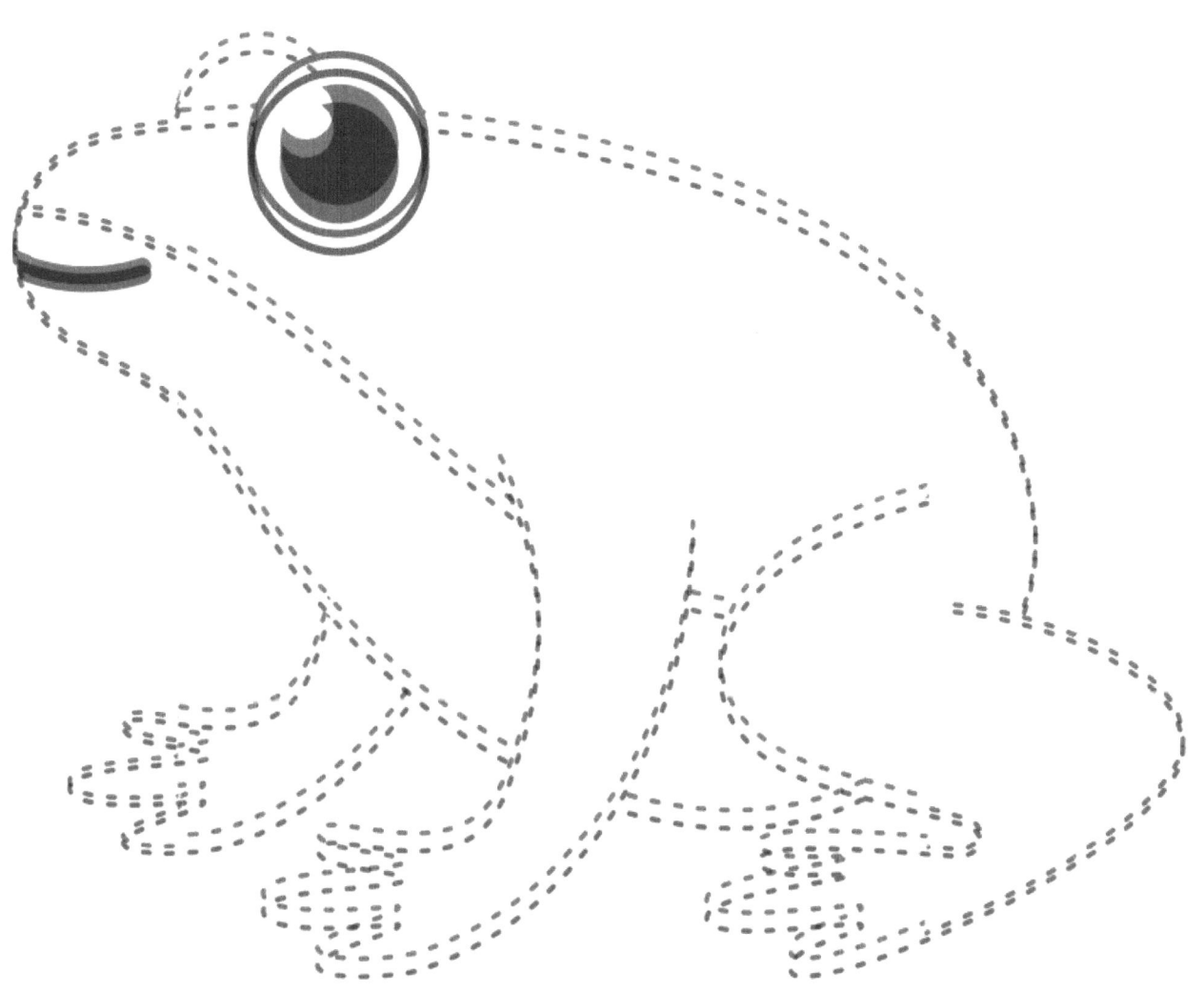

Giraffe Giraffe Giraffe

Giraffe Giraffe Giraffe

Giraffe Giraffe Giraffe

Giraffe Giraffe Giraffe

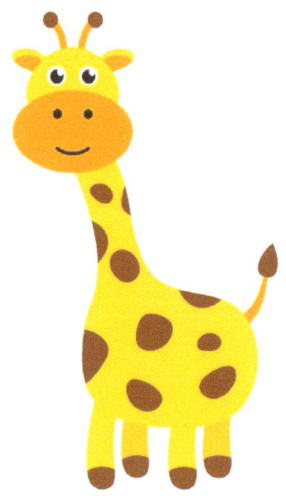

Giraffe

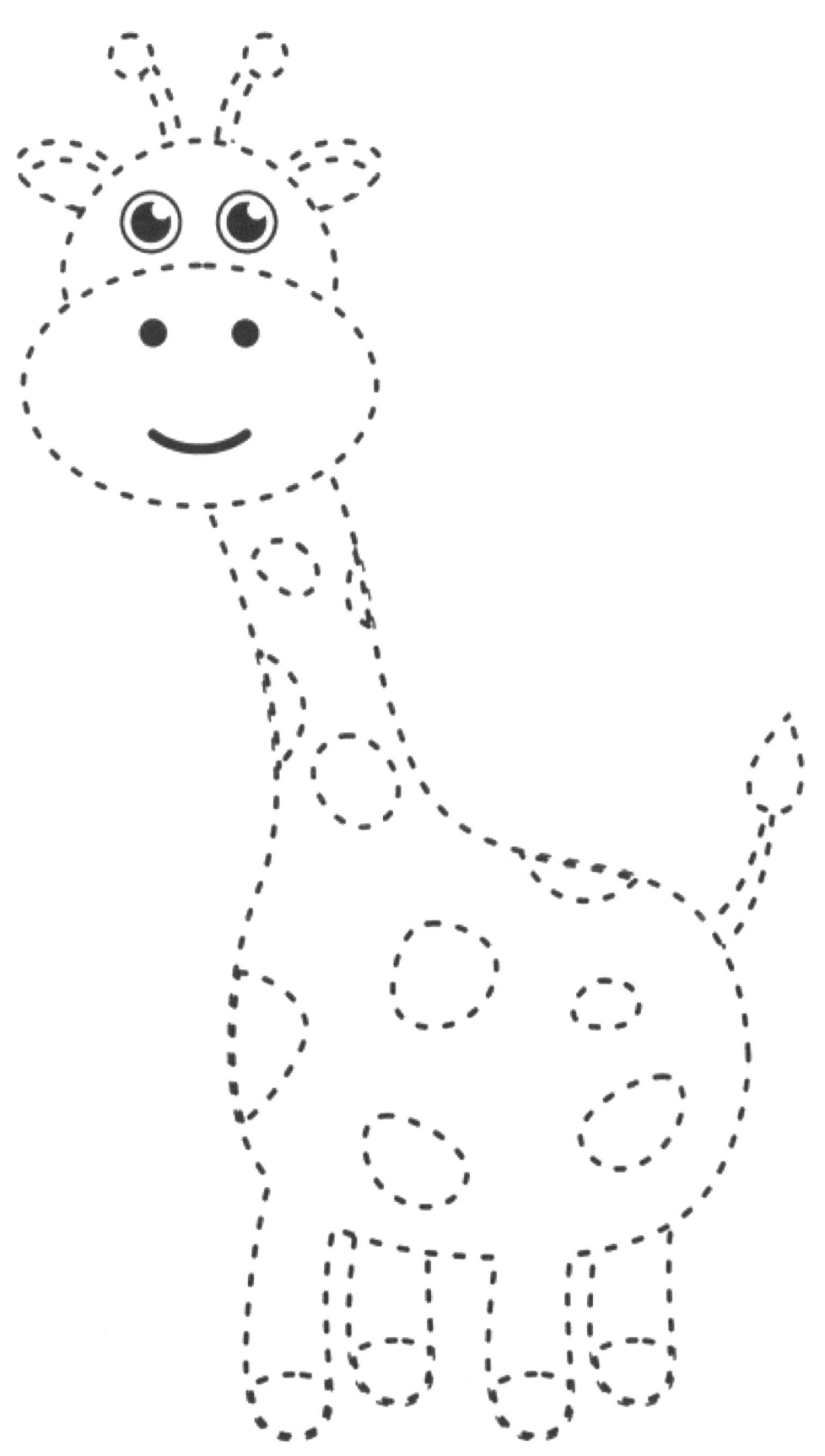

Grass Hopper

Grass Hopper

Grass Hopper

Grass Hopper

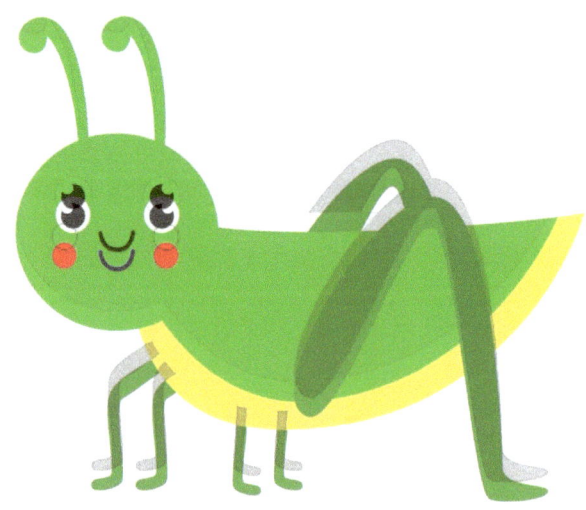

Grass Hopper

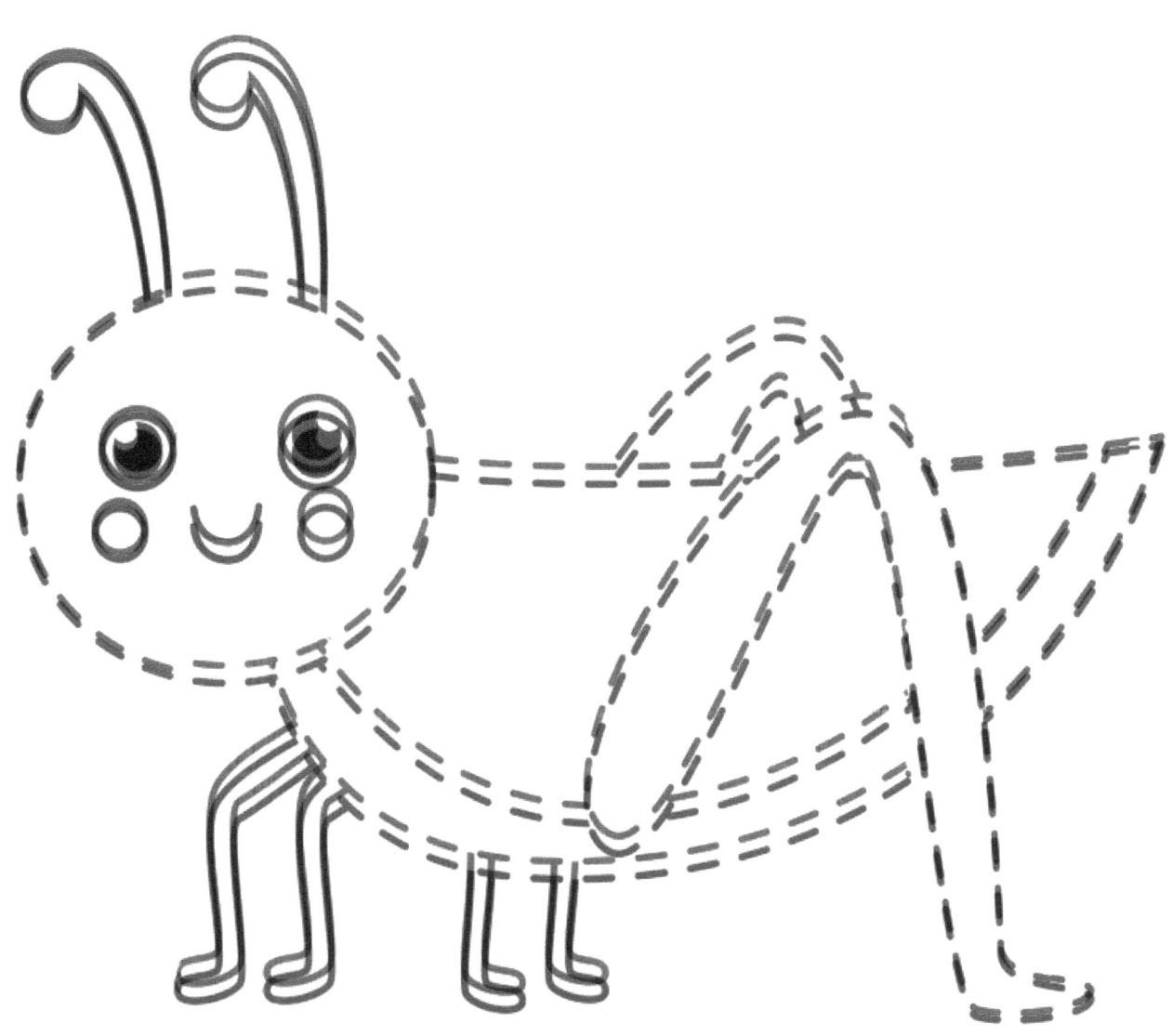

Hamburger   Hamburger

Hamburger   Hamburger

Hamburger   Hamburger

Hamburger   Hamburger

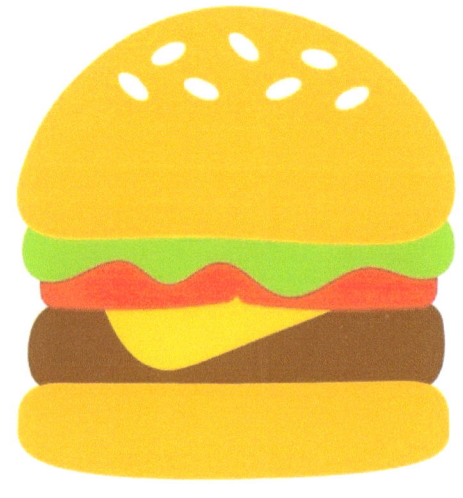

Hamburger

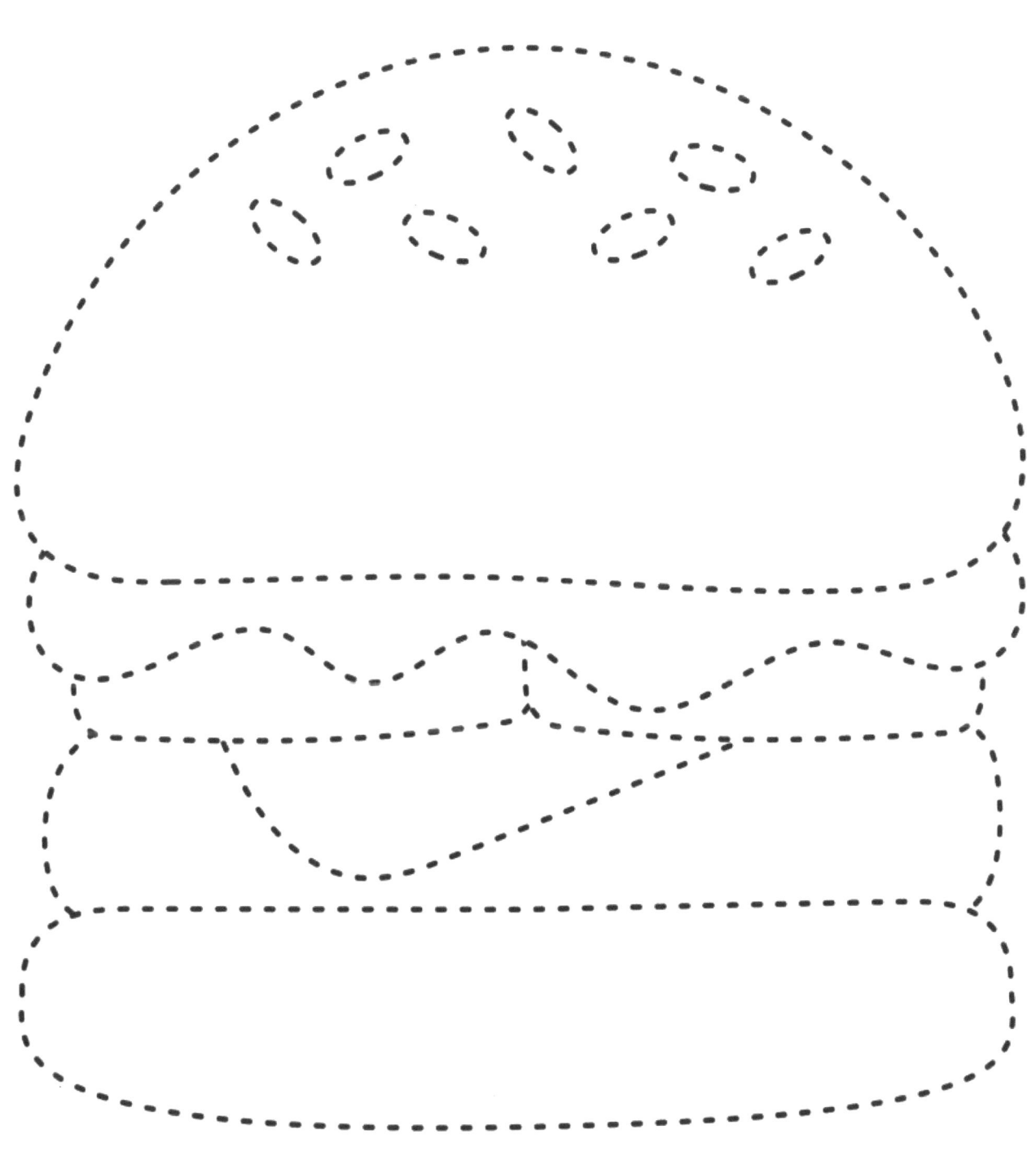

Helmet Helmet Helmet

Helmet Helmet Helmet

Helmet Helmet Helmet

Helmet Helmet Helmet

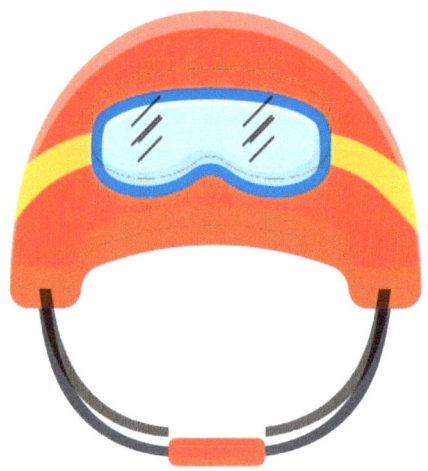

Helmut

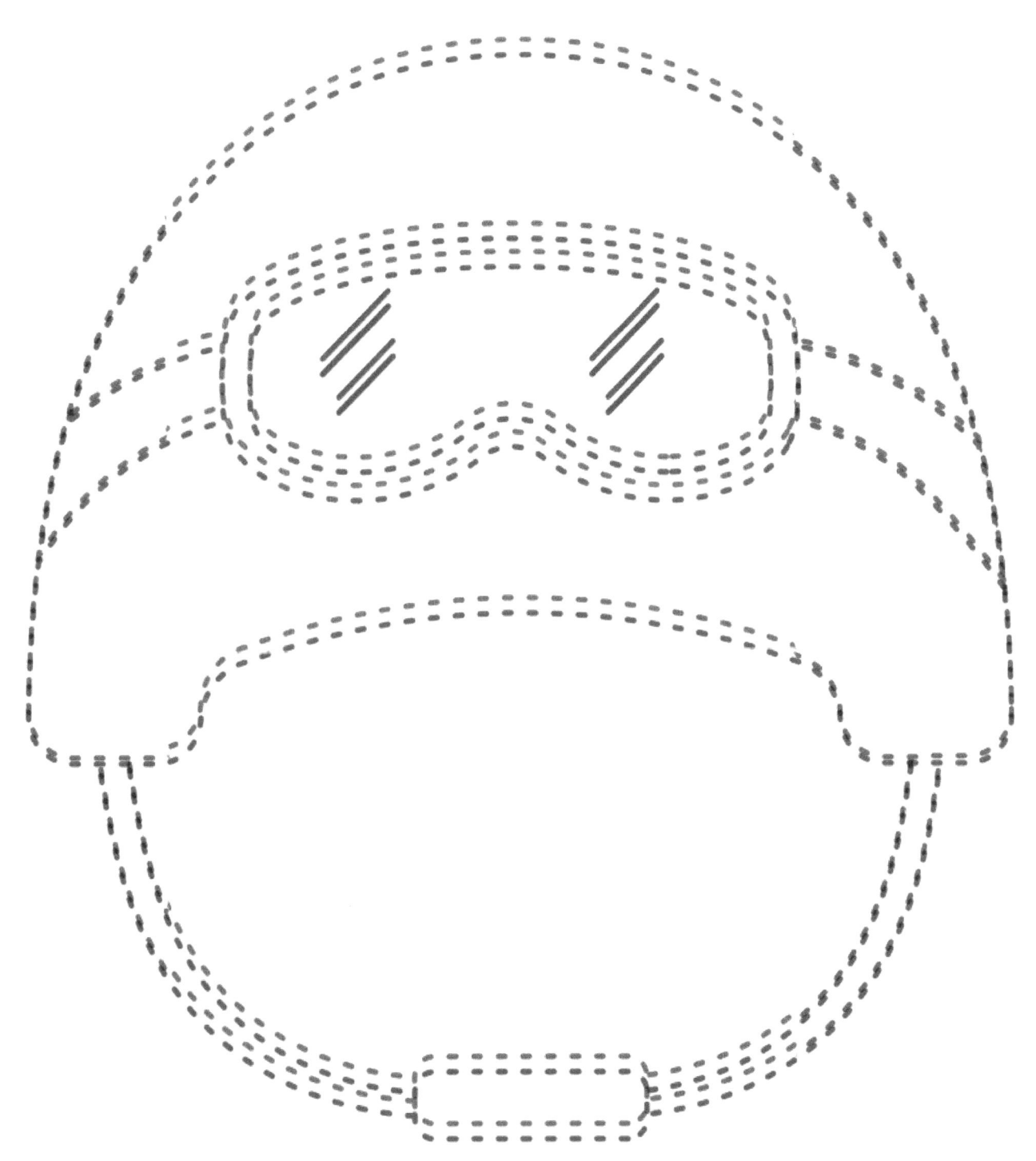

Ice Cream Ice Cream

Ice Cream Ice Cream

Ice Cream Ice Cream

Ice Cream Ice Cream

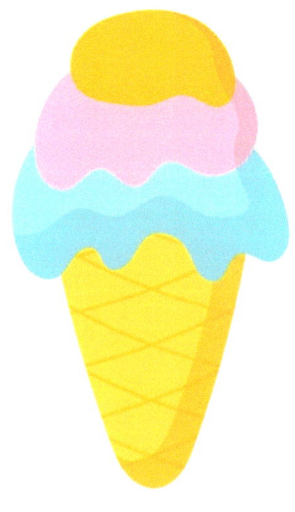

Ice Cream

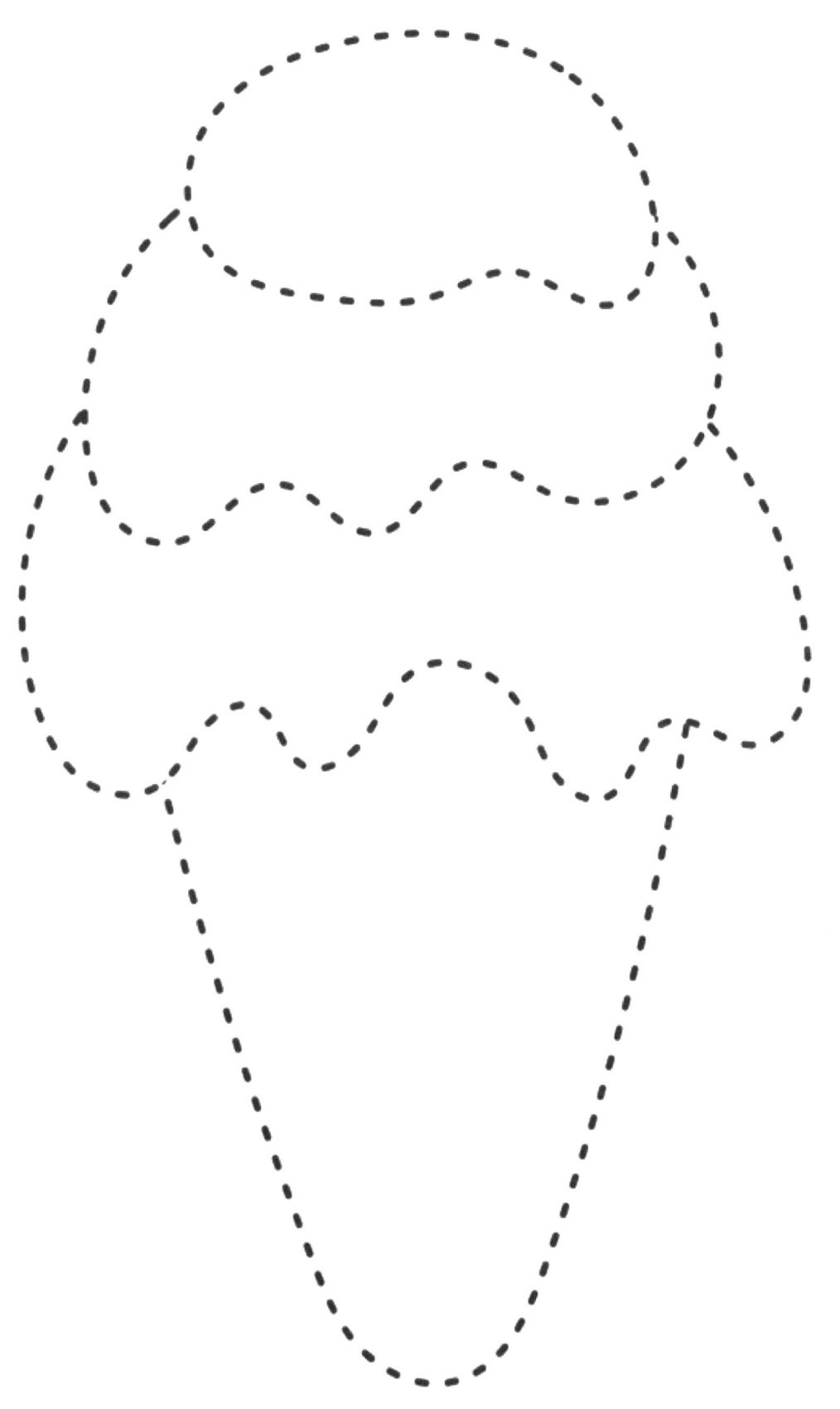

Lady Bug   Lady Bug

Lady Bug   Lady Bug

Lady Bug   Lady Bug

Lady Bug   Lady Bug

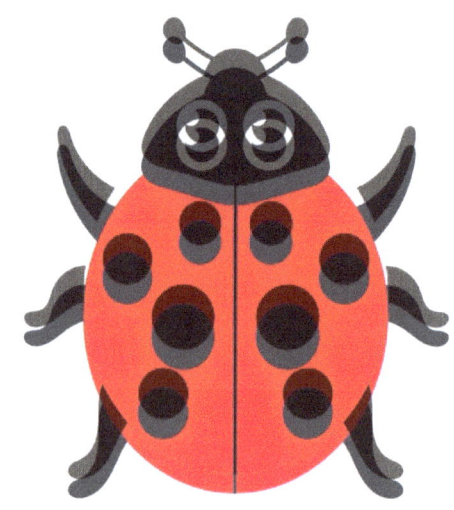

Ladybug

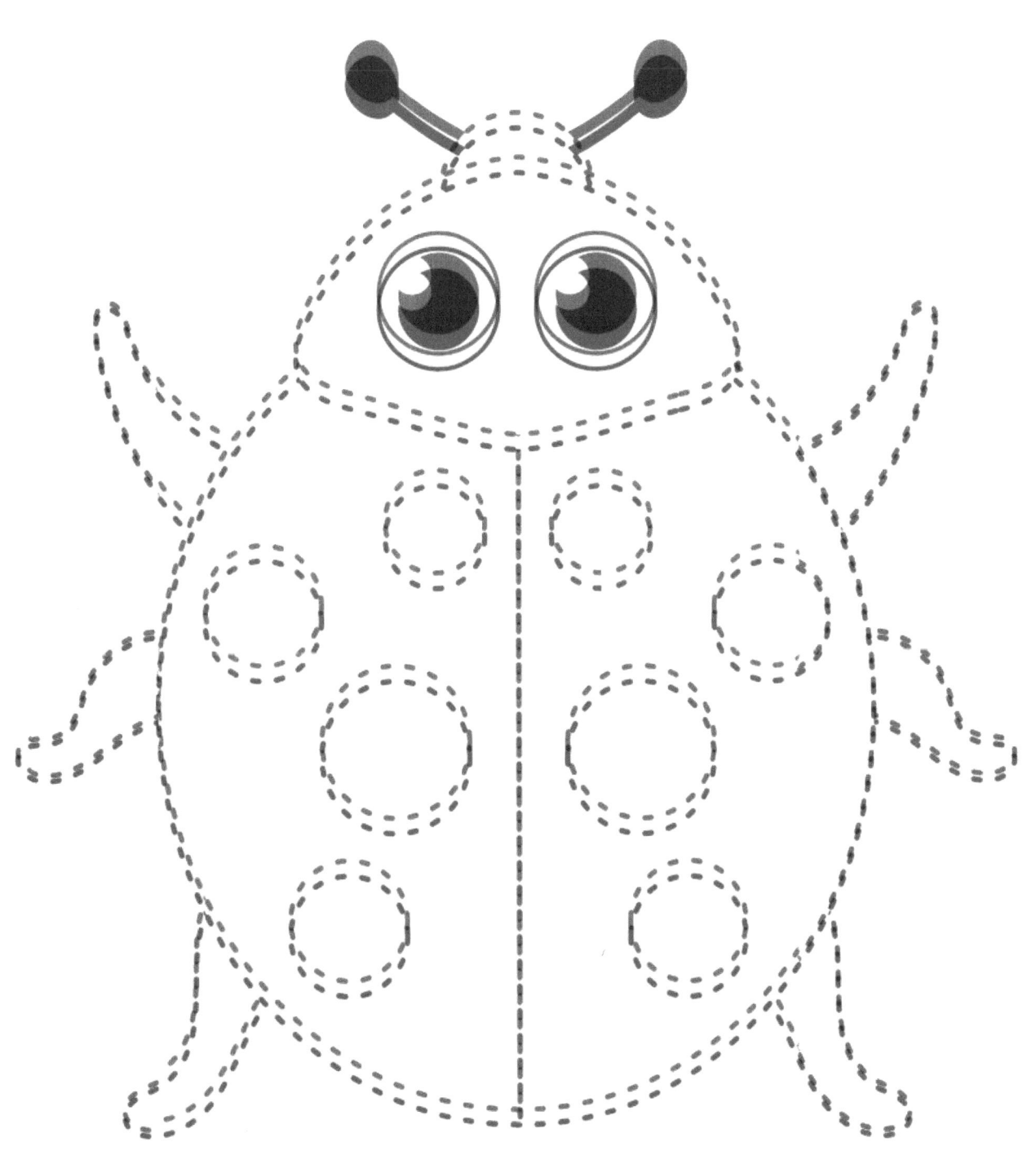

Magnifying Glass

Magnifying Glass

Magnifying Glass

Magnifying Glass

Magnifying Glass

Monkey Monkey Monkey

Monkey Monkey Monkey

Monkey Monkey Monkey

Monkey Monkey Monkey

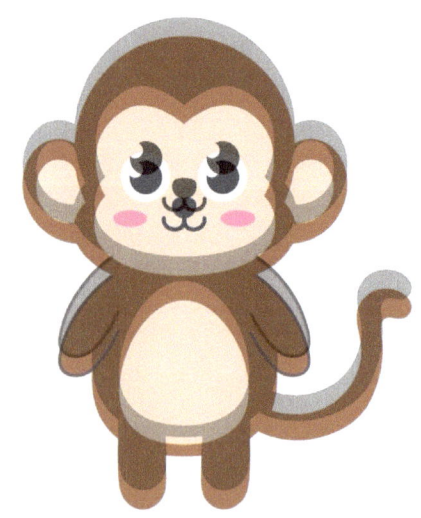

Monkey

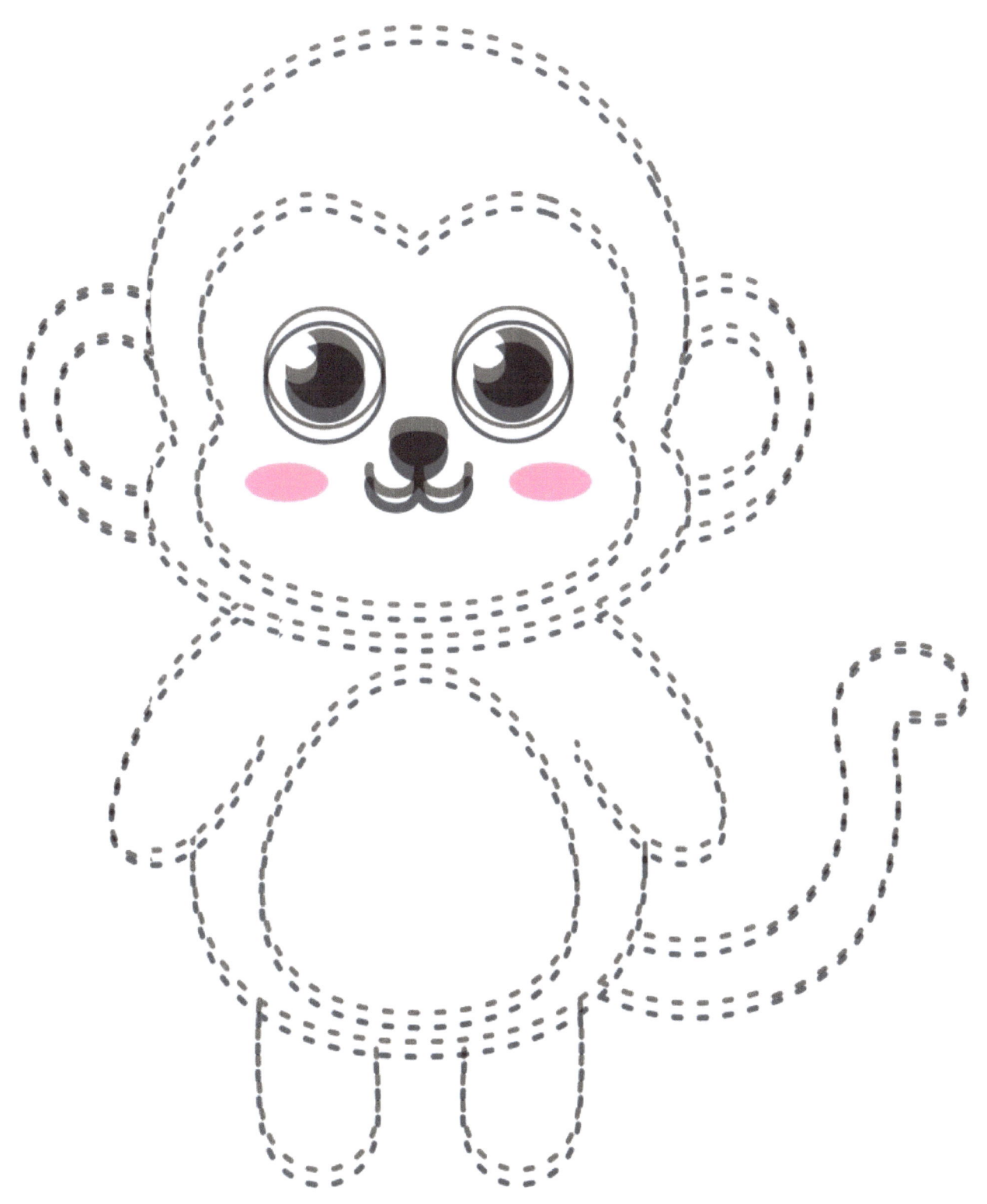

Mushroom   Mushroom

Mushroom   Mushroom

Mushroom   Mushroom

Mushroom   Mushroom

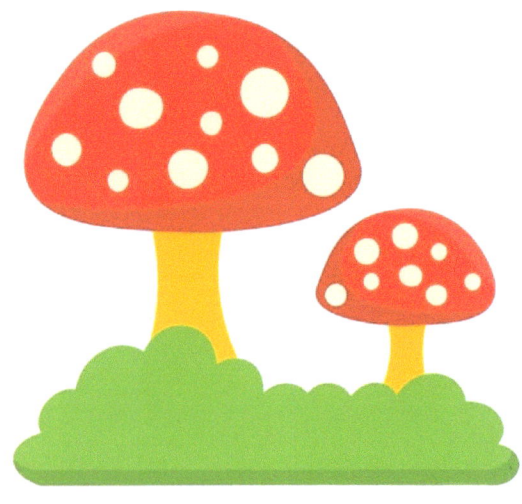

Mushroom

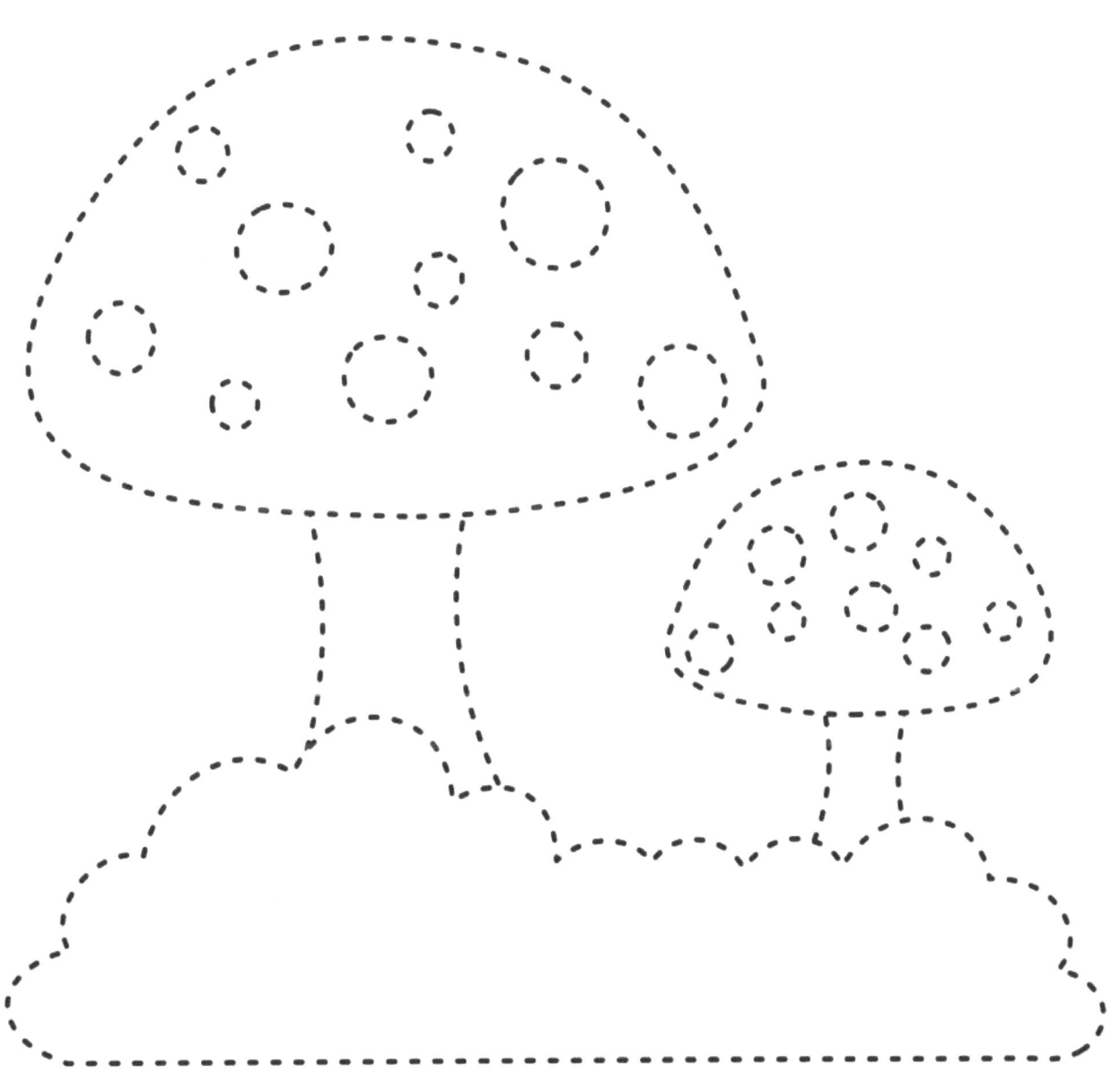

Music Note   Music Note

Music Note   Music Note

Music Note   Music Note

Music Note   Music Note

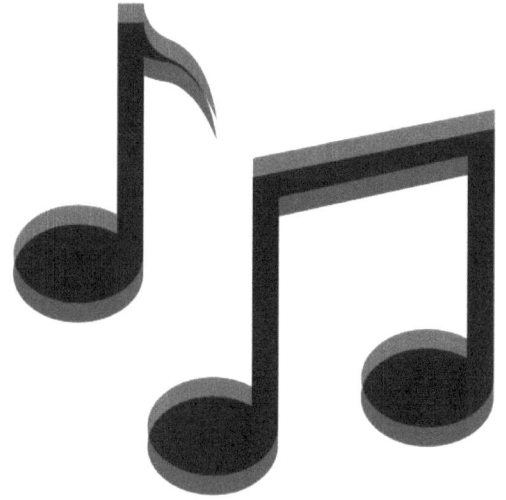

Musical Note

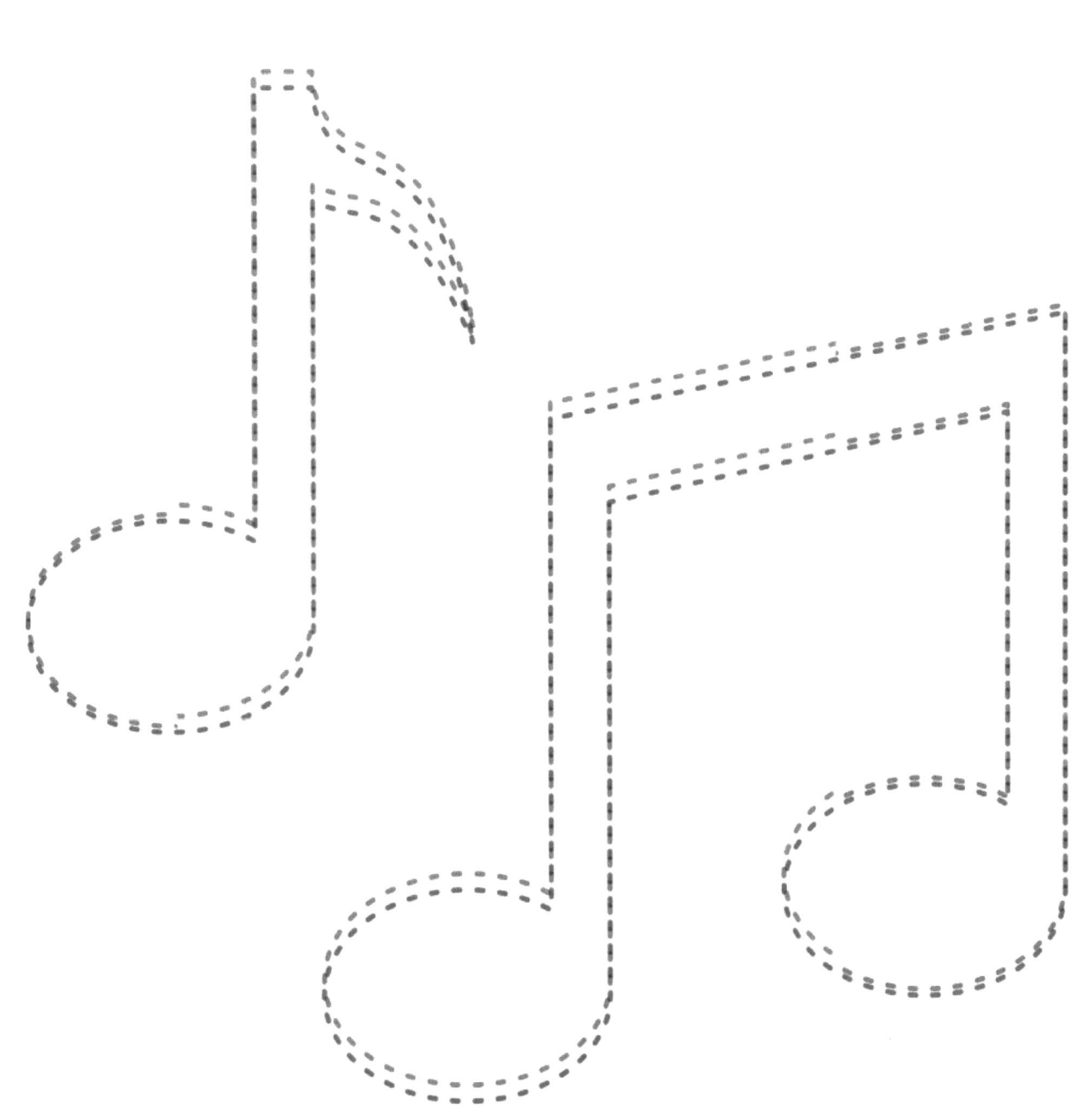

Owl   Owl   Owl   Owl

Owl   Owl   Owl   Owl

Owl   Owl   Owl   Owl

Owl   Owl   Owl   Owl

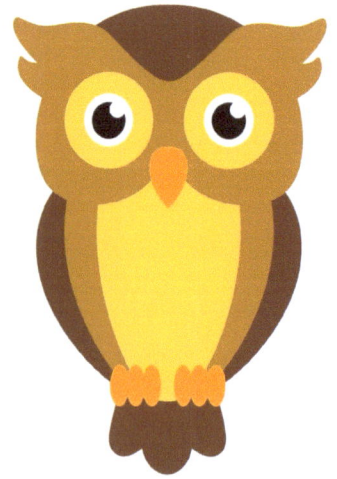

Owl

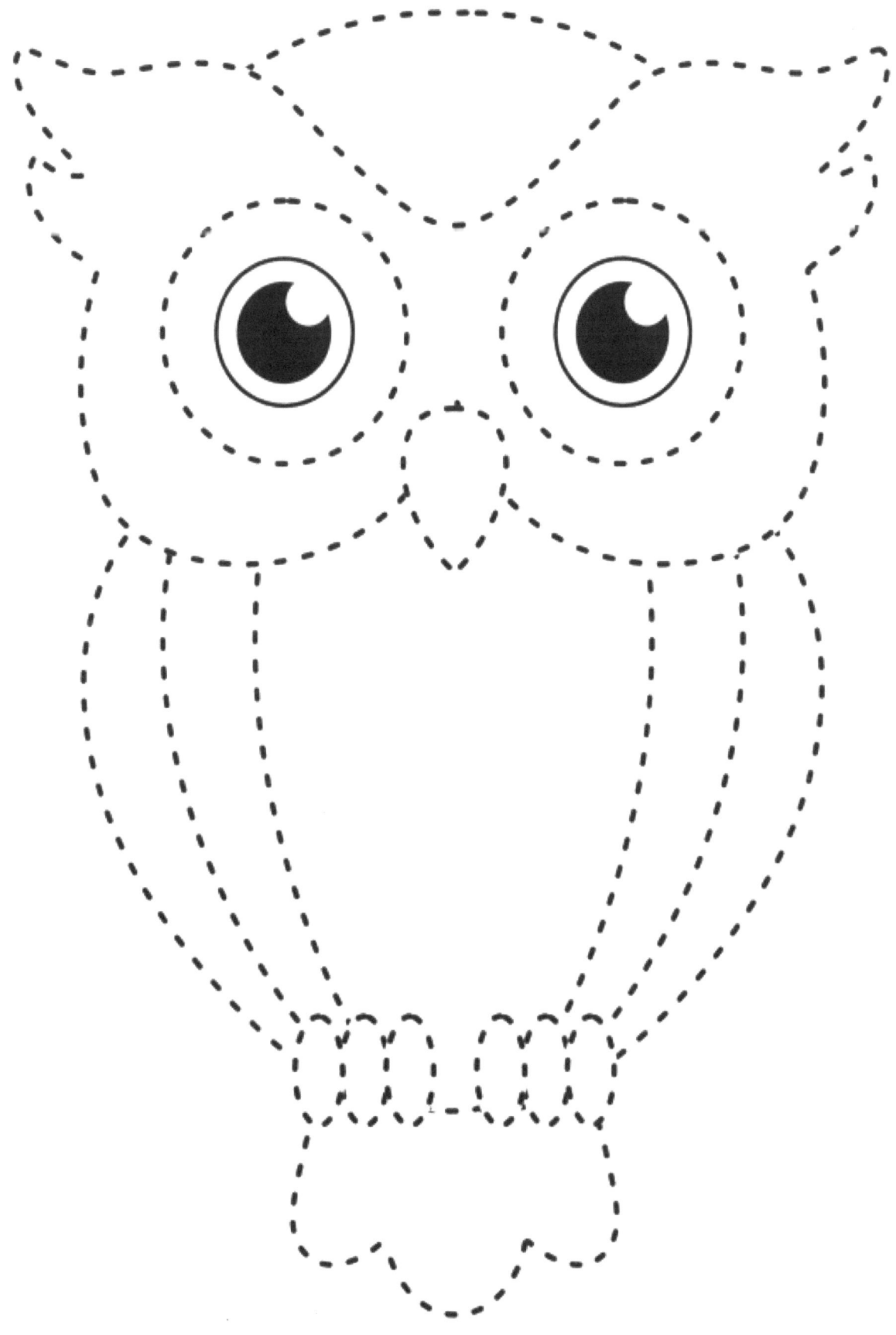

Paint Brush   Paint Brush

Paint Brush   Paint Brush

Paint Brush   Paint Brush

Paint Brush   Paint Brush

Paint Brush

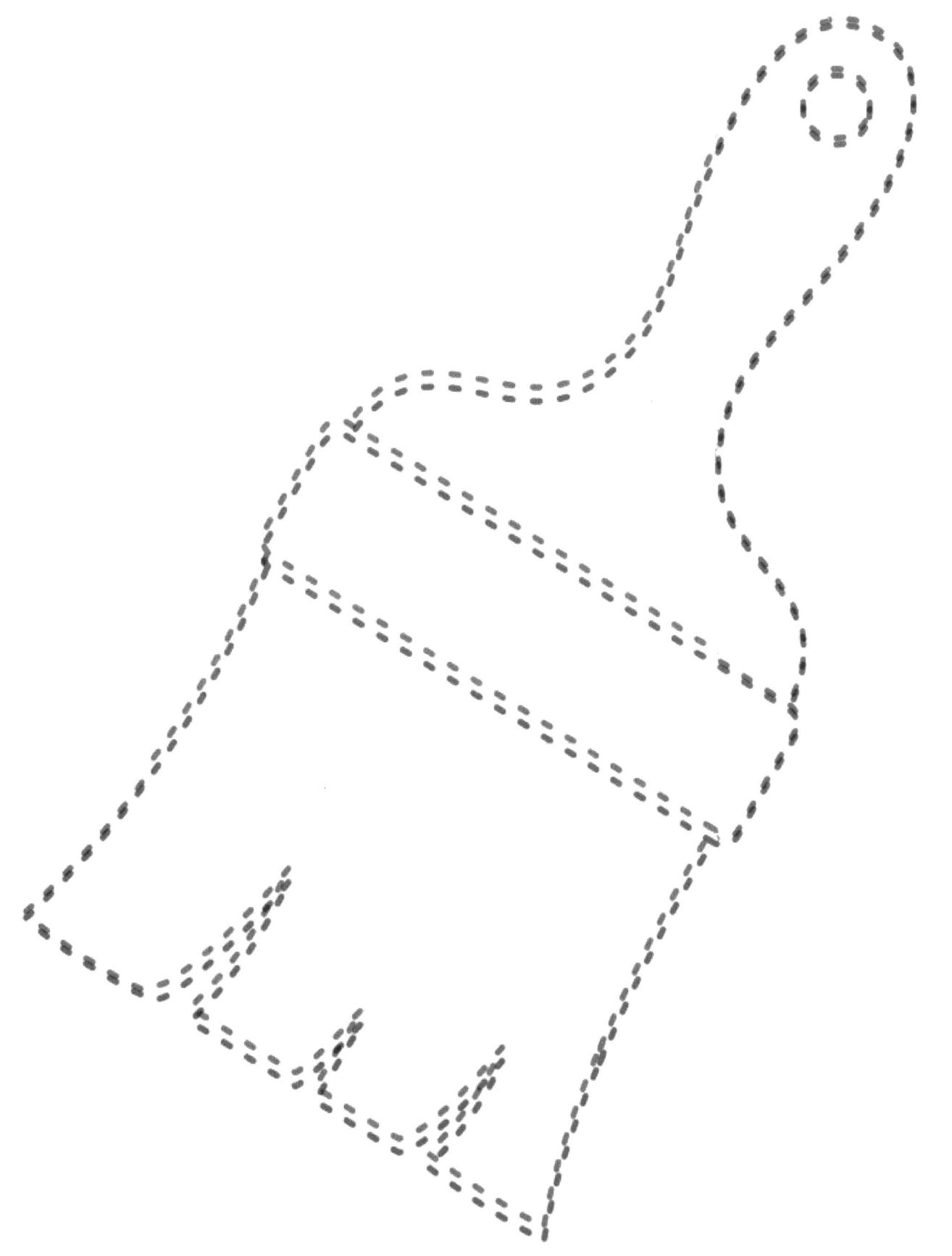

Paint Palette   Paint Palette

Paint Palette   Paint Palette

Paint Palette   Paint Palette

Paint Palette   Paint Palette

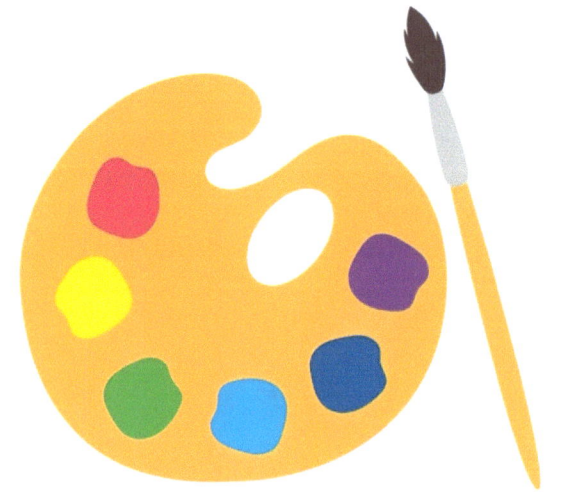

Paint Palette

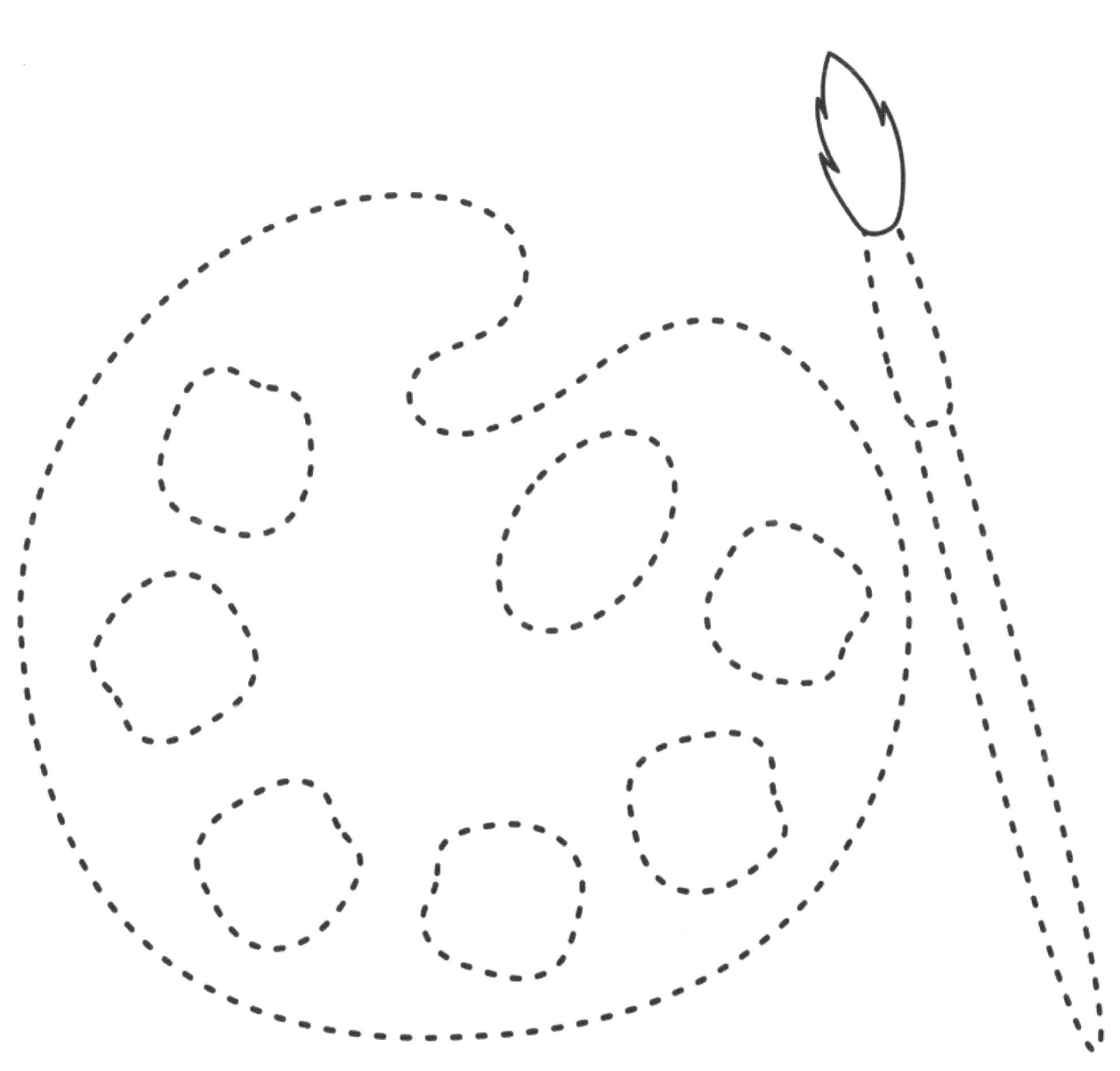

Paper Windmill

Paper Windmill

Paper Windmill

Paper Windmill

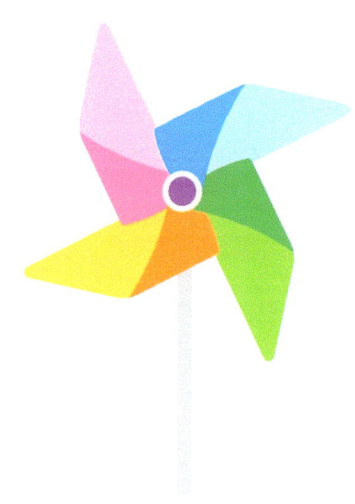

Paper Windmill

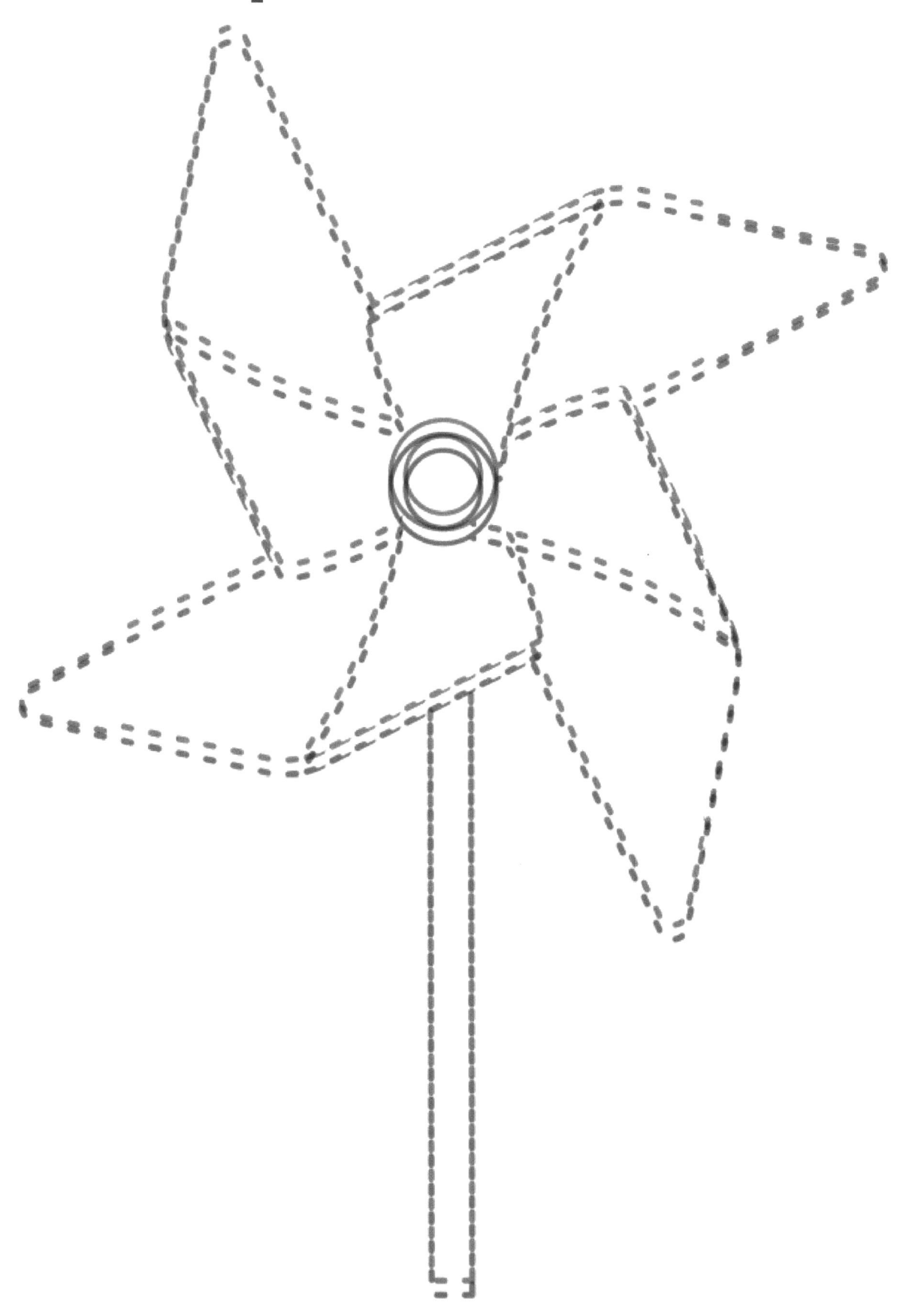

Penguin Penguin Penguin

Penguin Penguin Penguin

Penguin Penguin Penguin

Penguin Penguin Penguin

Penguin

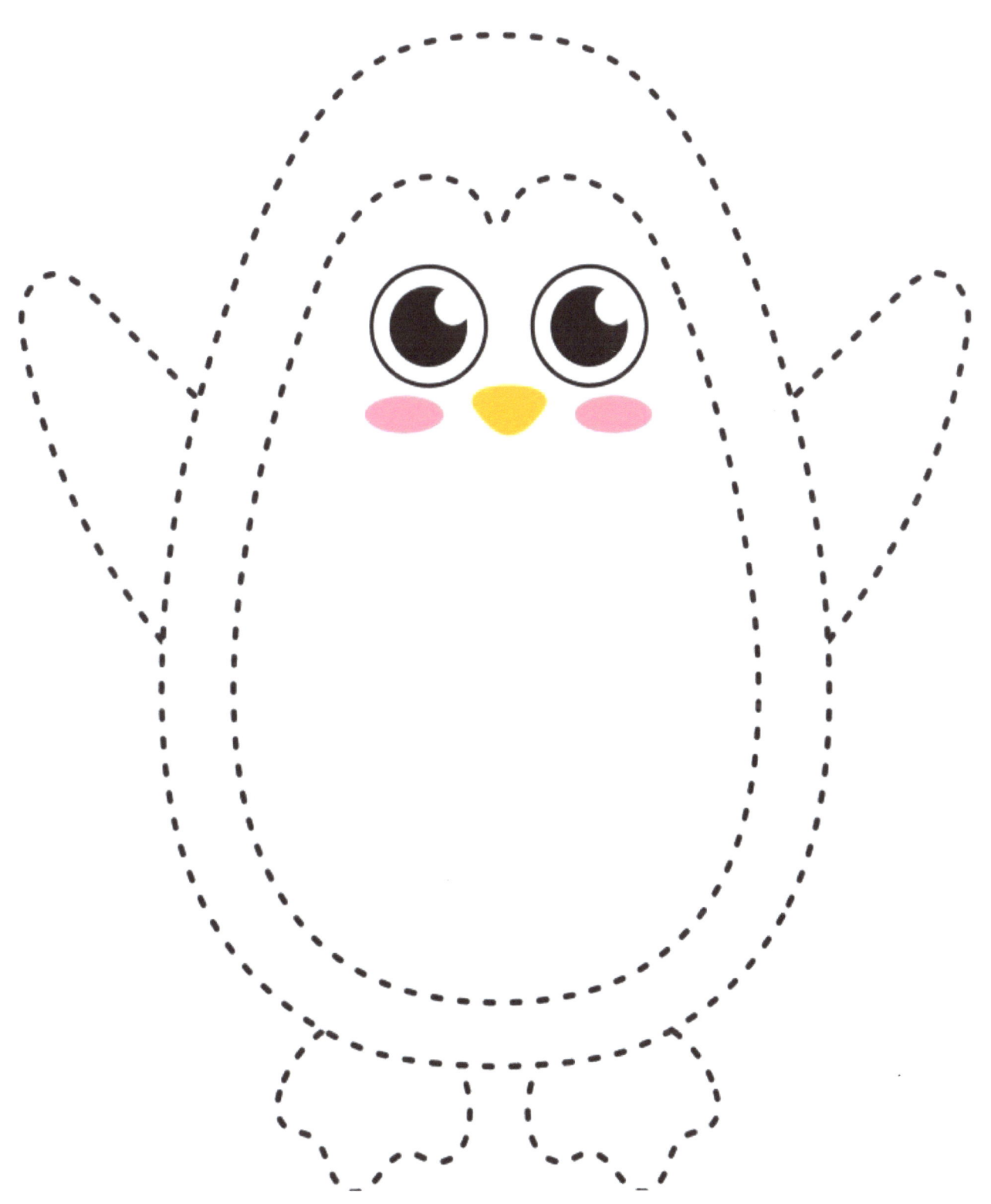

Pizza Pizza Pizza

Pizza Pizza Pizza

Pizza Pizza Pizza

Pizza Pizza Pizza

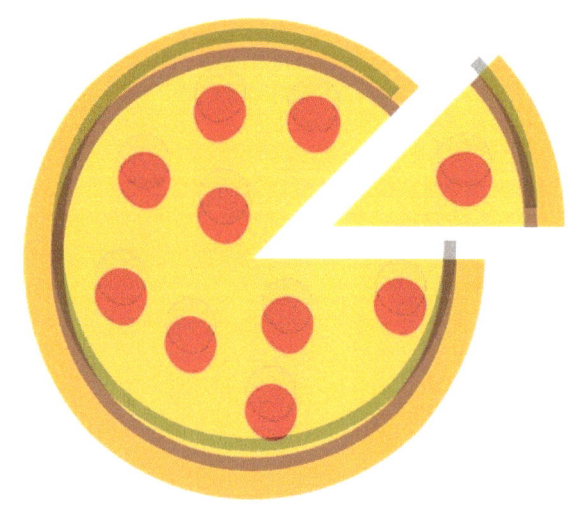

Pizza

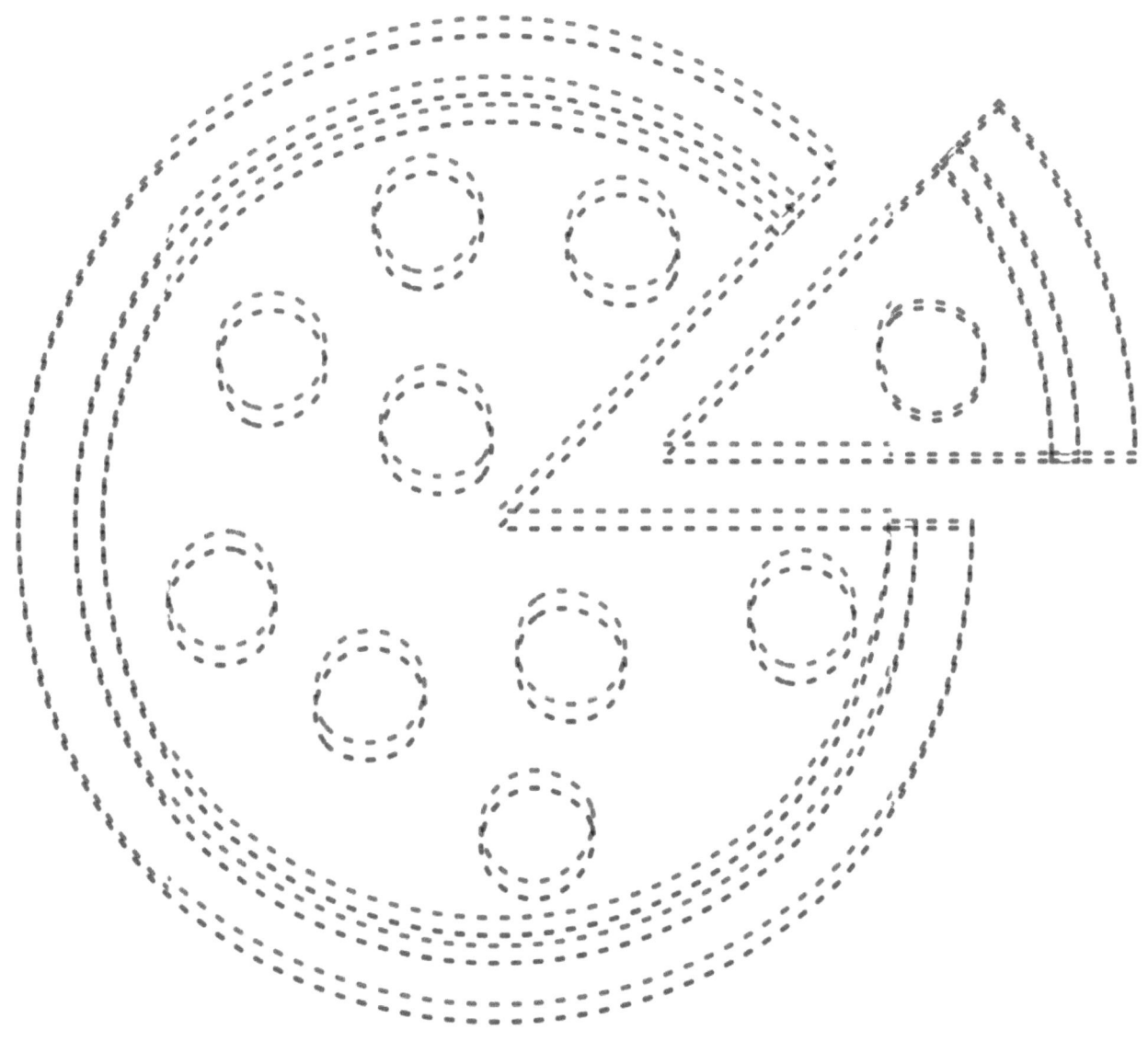

Present Present Present

Present Present Present

Present Present Present

Present Present Present

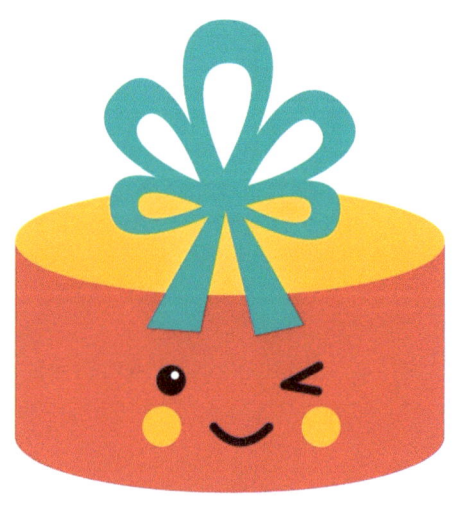

Present

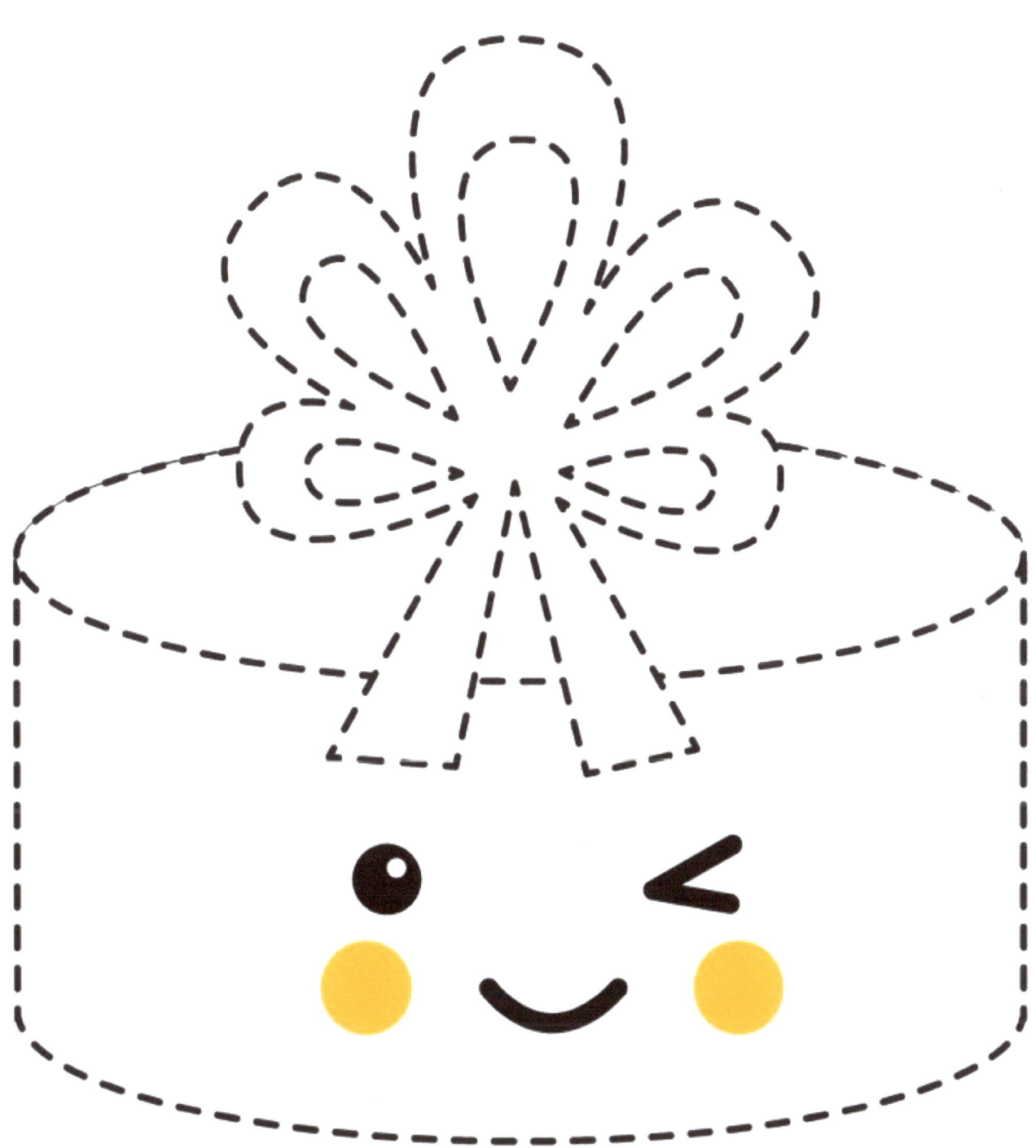

Shoes   Shoes   Shoes

Shoes   Shoes   Shoes

Shoes   Shoes   Shoes

Shoes   Shoes   Shoes

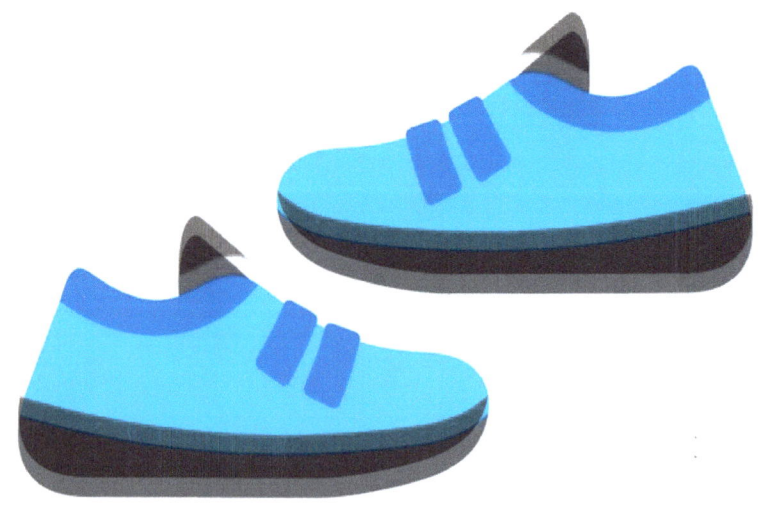

Shoes

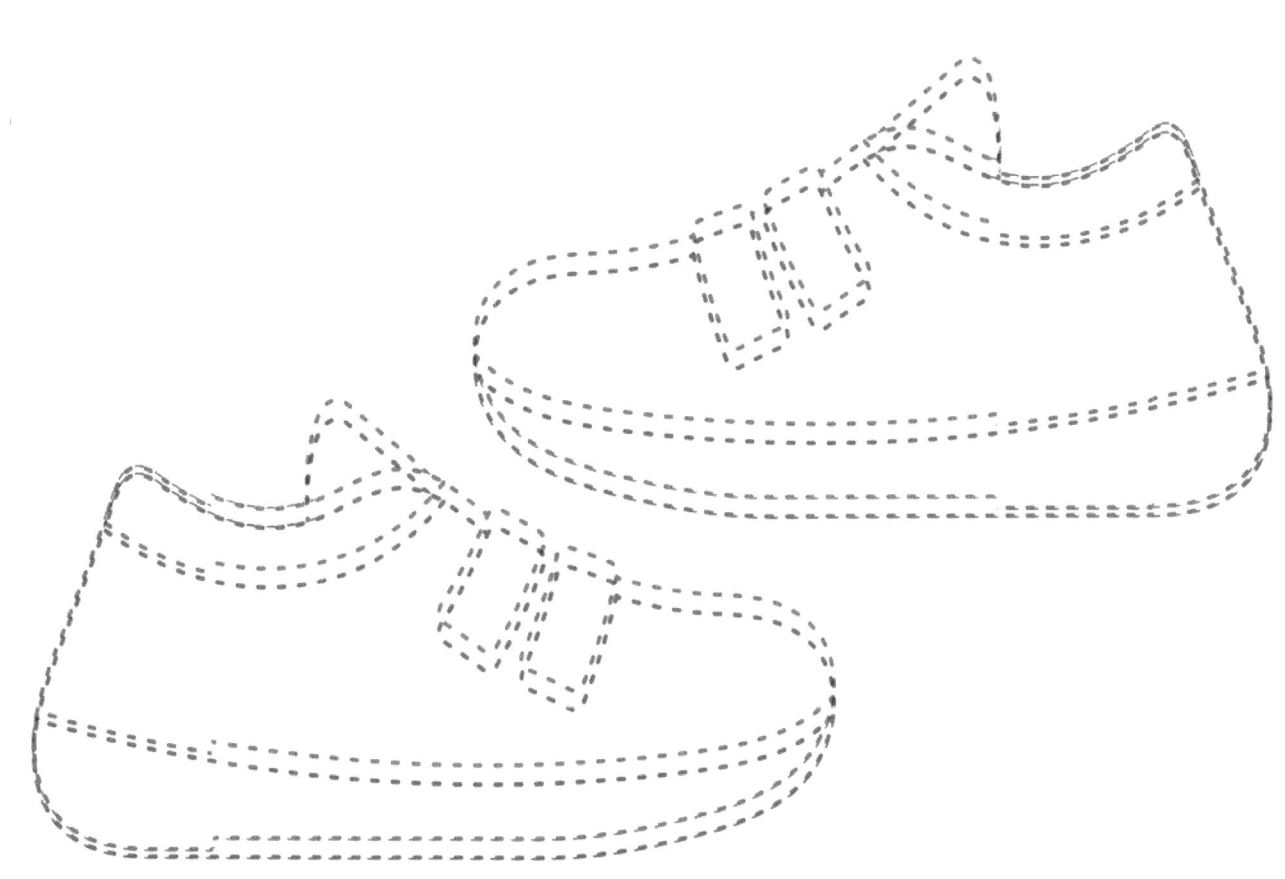

Star Star Star Star

Star Star Star Star

Star Star Star Star

Star Star Star Star

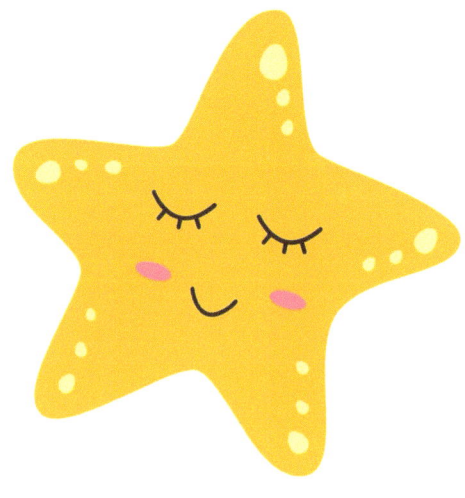

Star

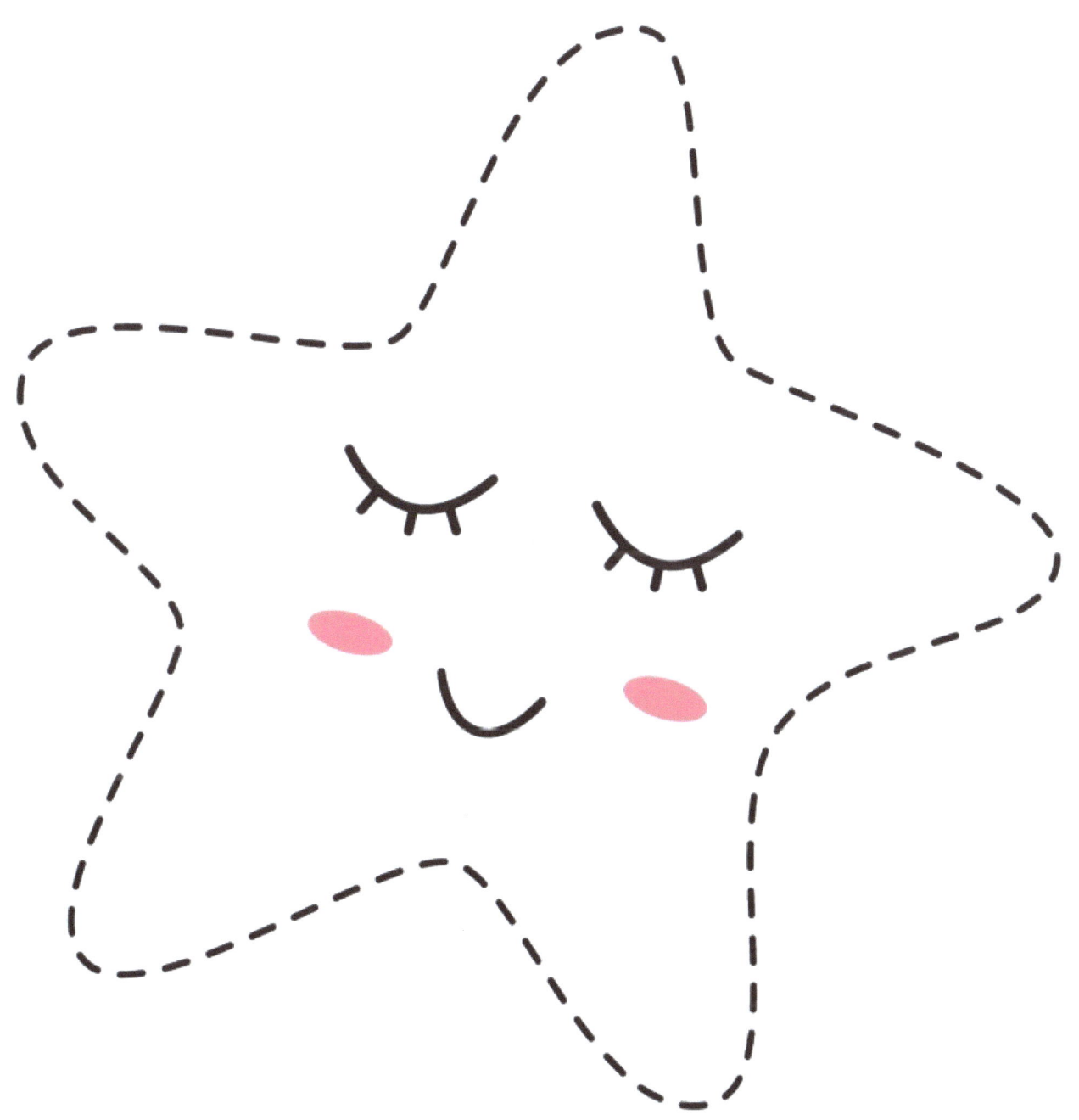

Stork   Stork   Stork

Stork   Stork   Stork

Stork   Stork   Stork

Stork   Stork   Stork

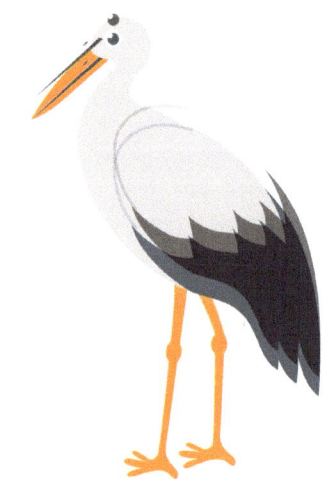

Stork

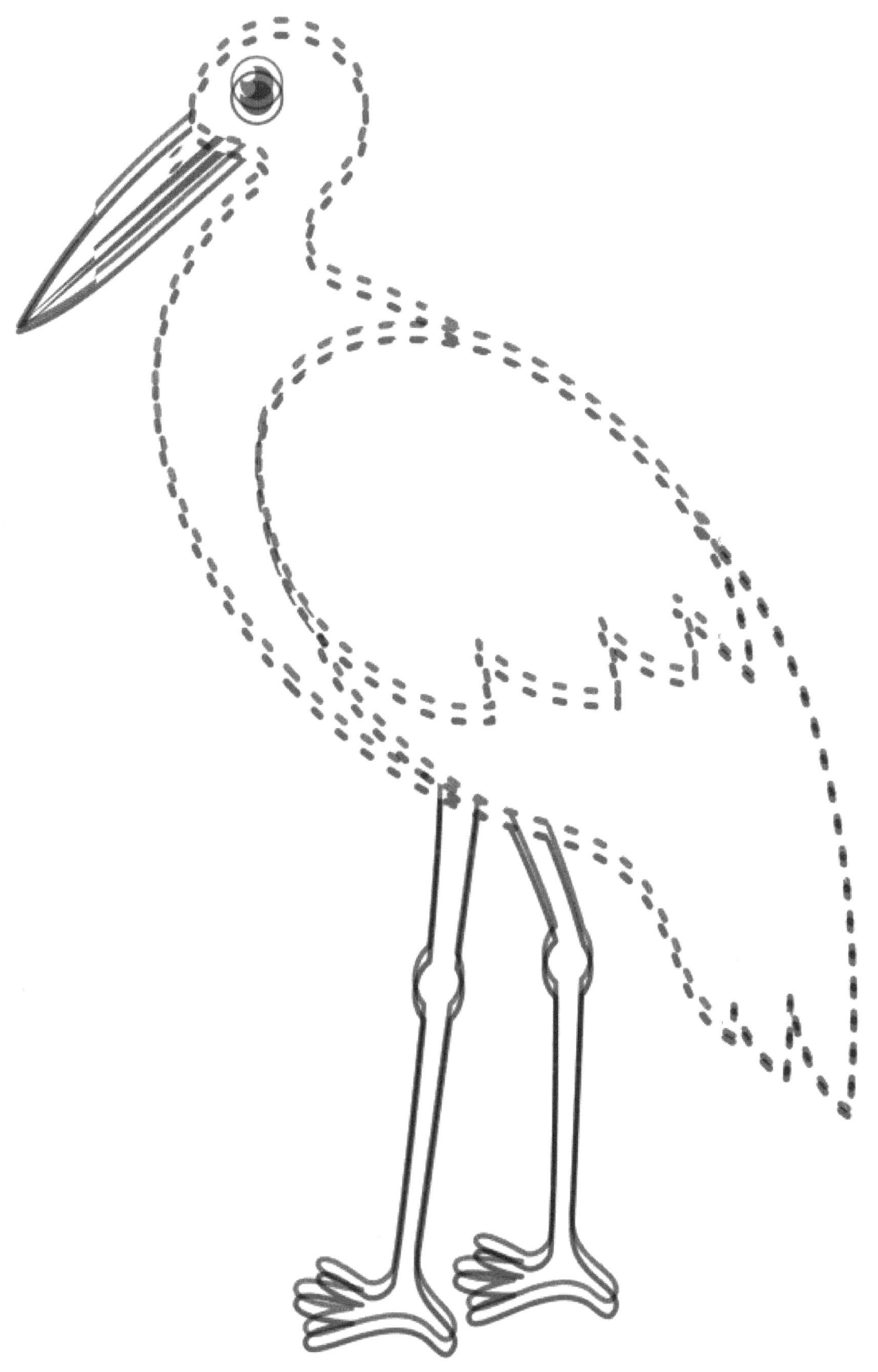

Strawberry

Strawberry

Strawberry

Strawberry

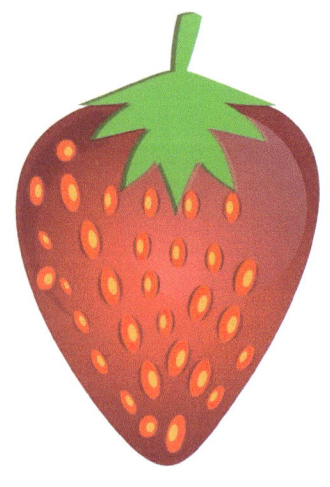

Strawberry

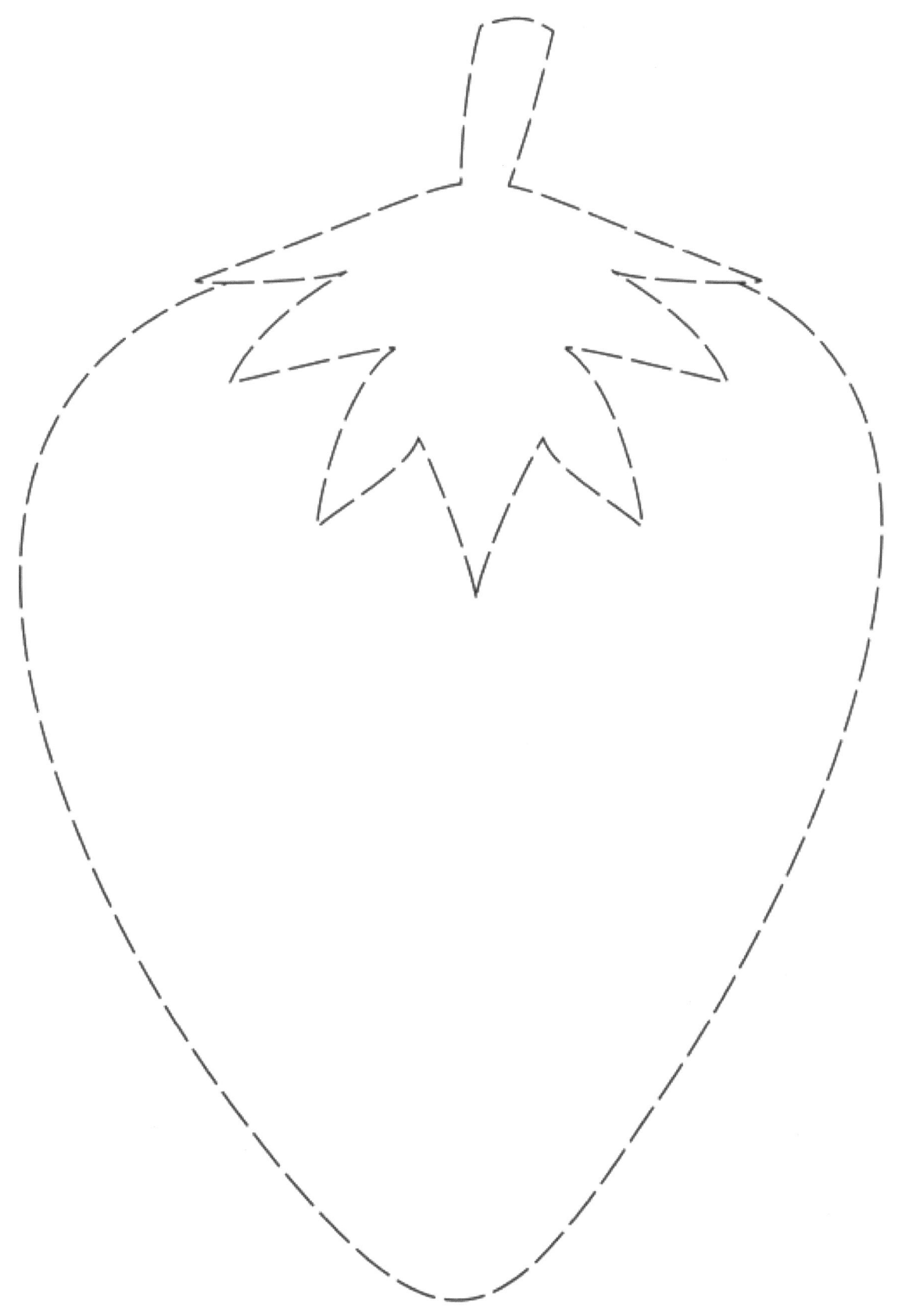

Sunflower Sunflower

Sunflower Sunflower

Sunflower Sunflower

Sunflower Sunflower

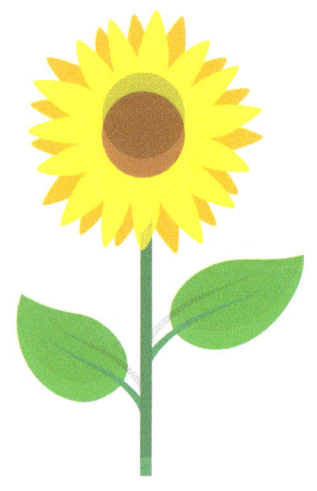

Sunflower

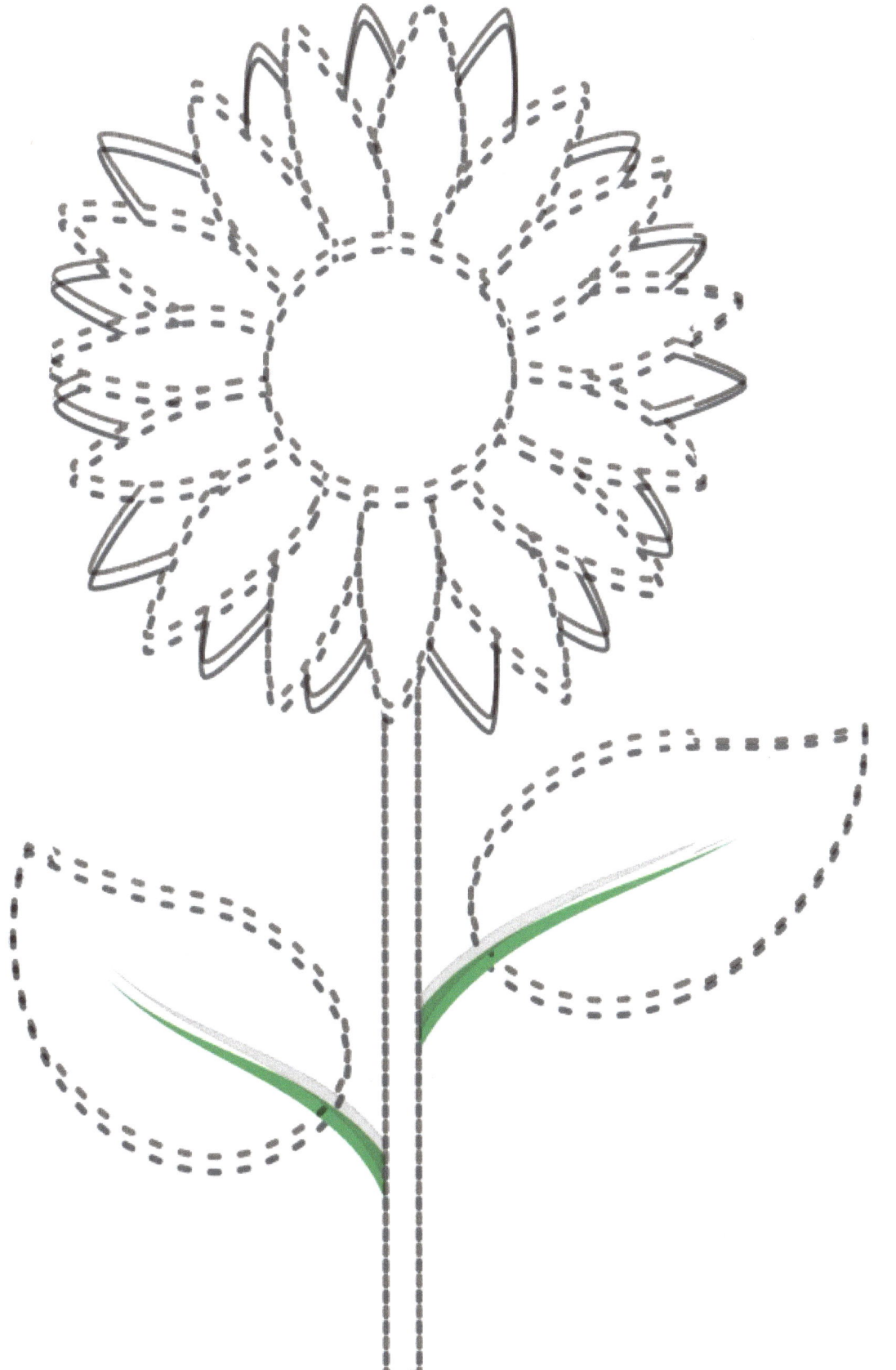

Telephone   Telephone

Telephone   Telephone

Telephone   Telephone

Telephone   Telephone

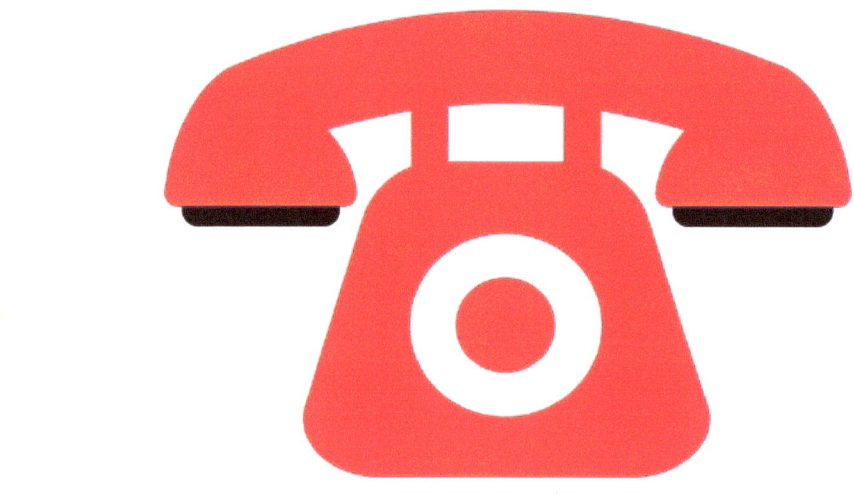

Telephone

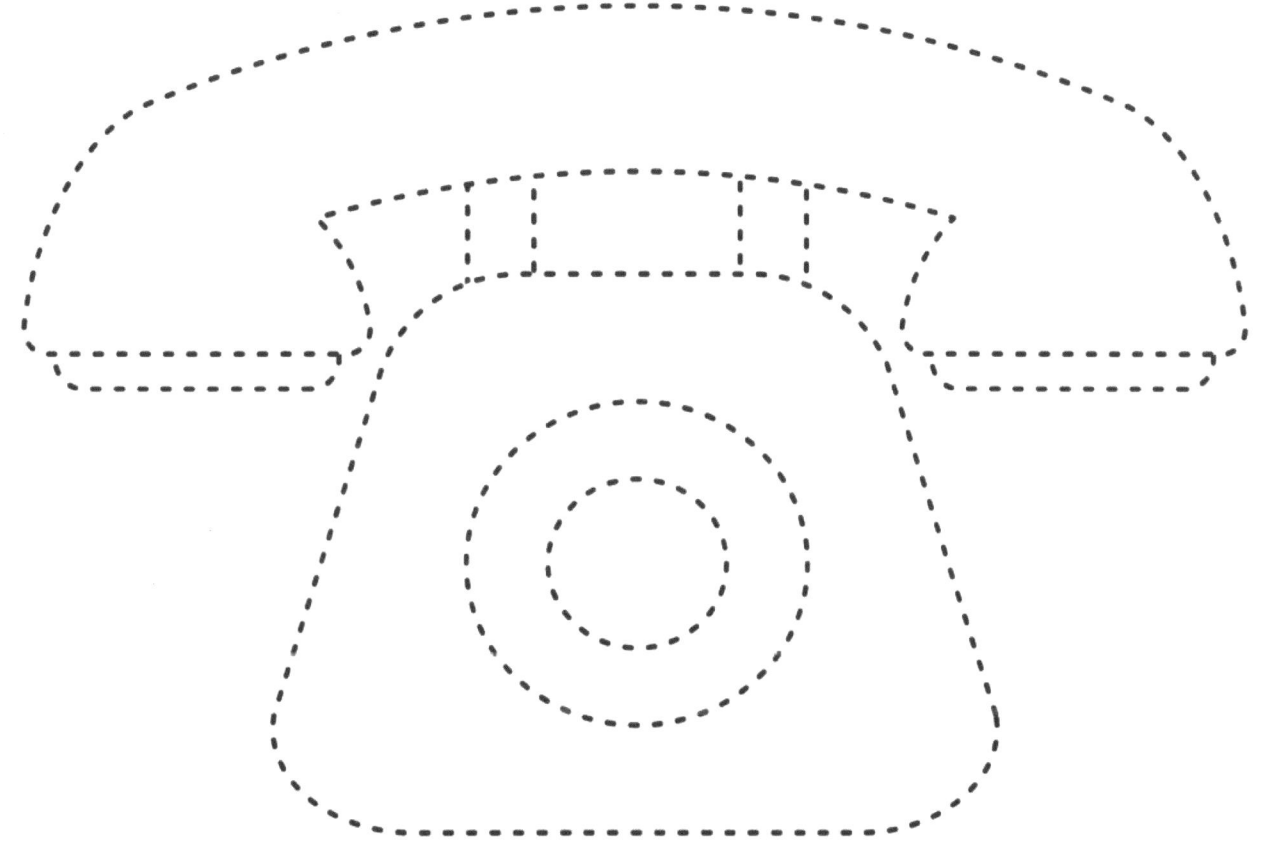

Tie   Tie   Tie   Tie

Tie   Tie   Tie   Tie

Tie   Tie   Tie   Tie

Tie   Tie   Tie   Tie

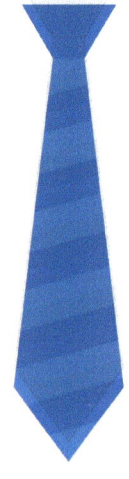

Tie

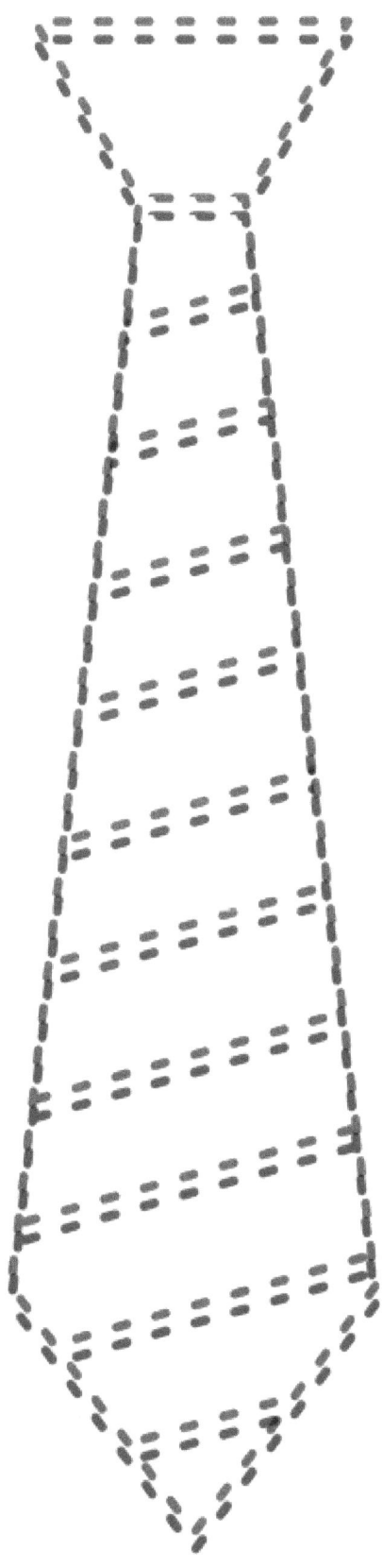

Train   Train   Train

Train   Train   Train

Train   Train   Train

Train   Train   Train

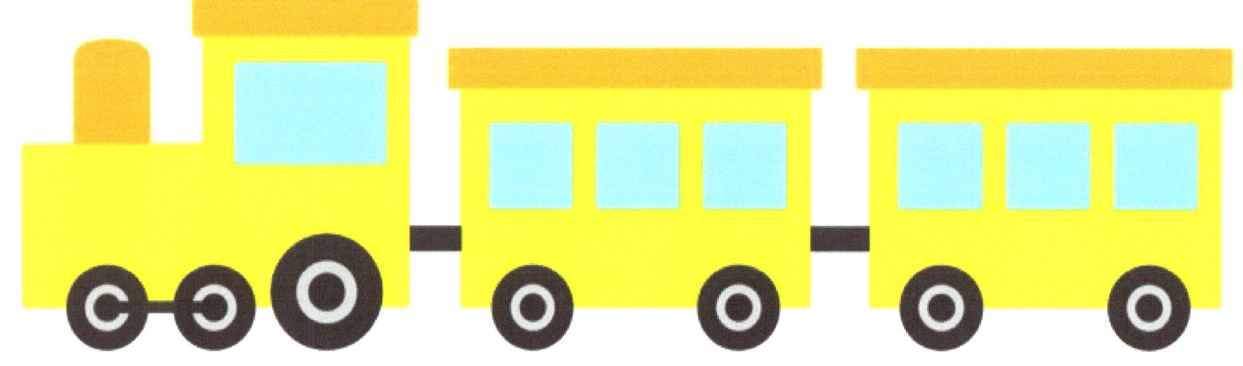

Train

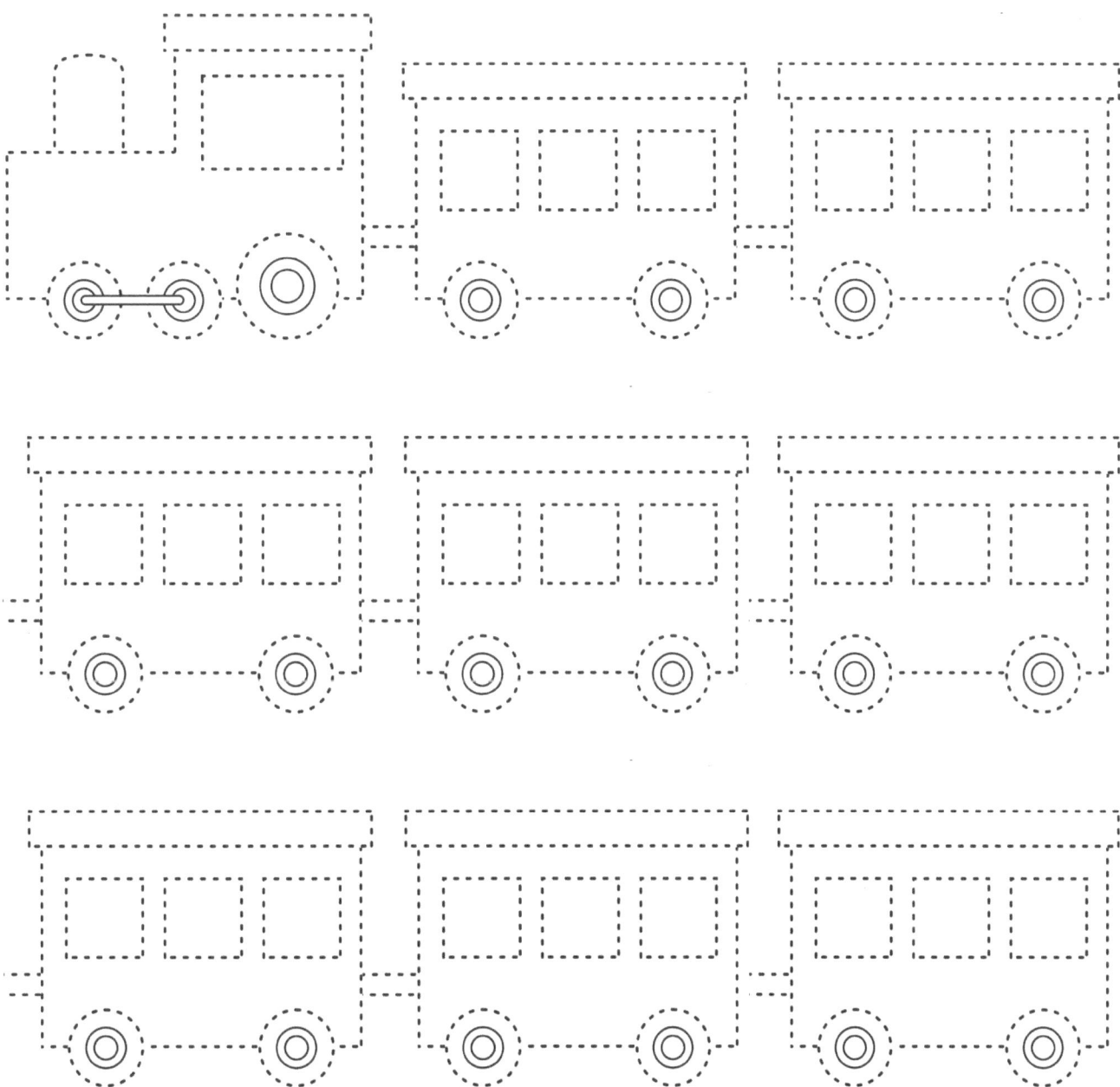

Trophy   Trophy   Trophy

Trophy   Trophy   Trophy

Trophy   Trophy   Trophy

Trophy   Trophy   Trophy

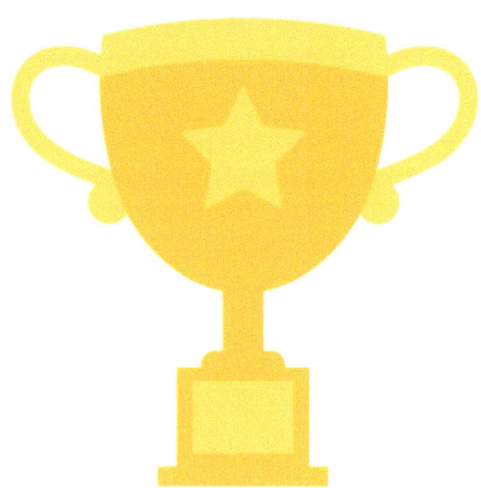

Trophy

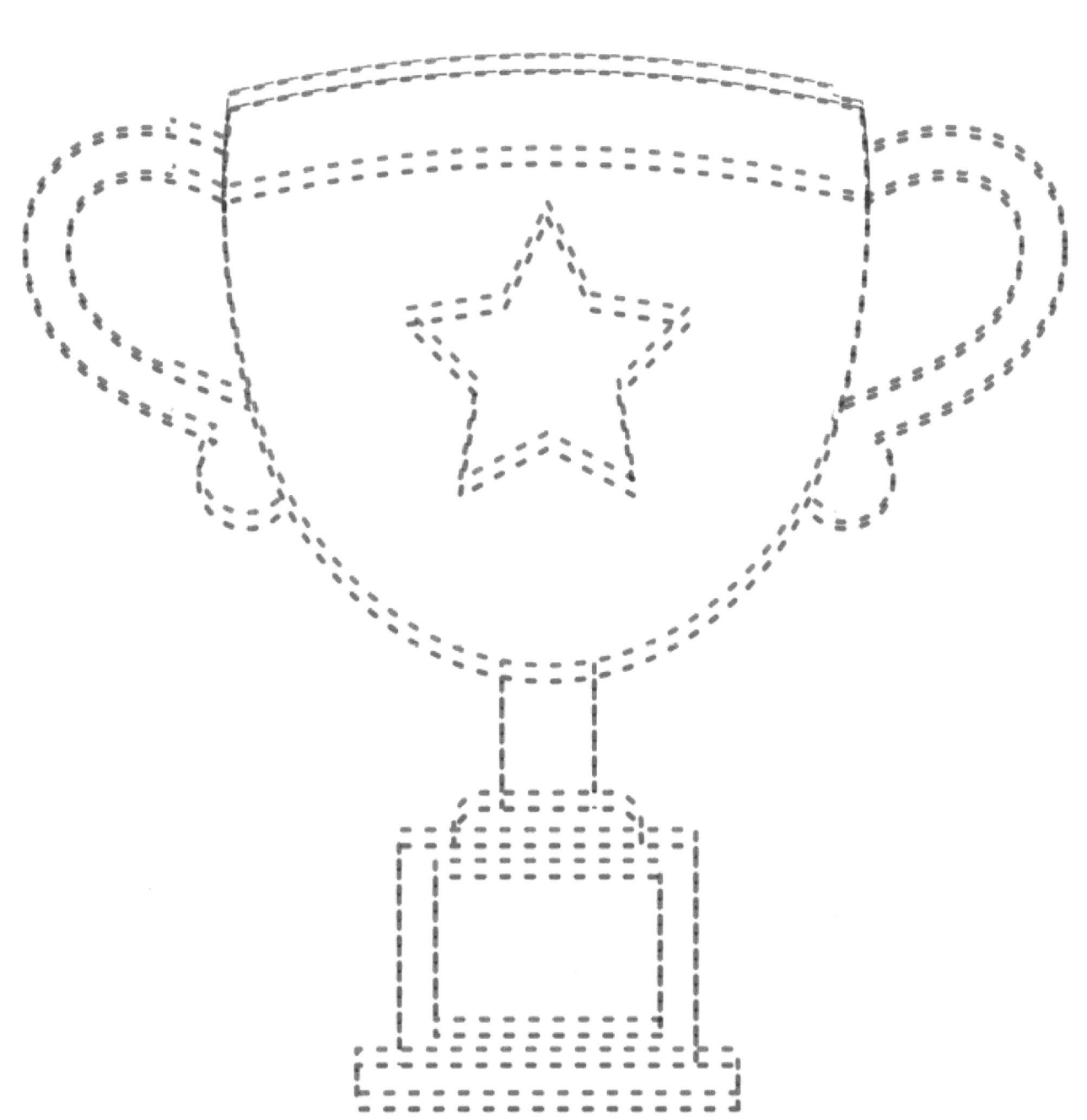

Watermelon Watermelon

Watermelon Watermelon

Watermelon Watermelon

Watermelon Watermelon

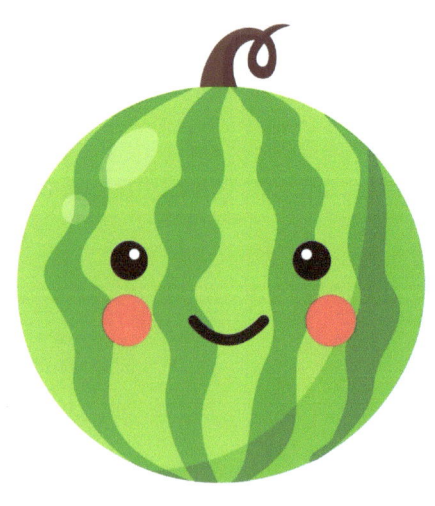

Watermelon

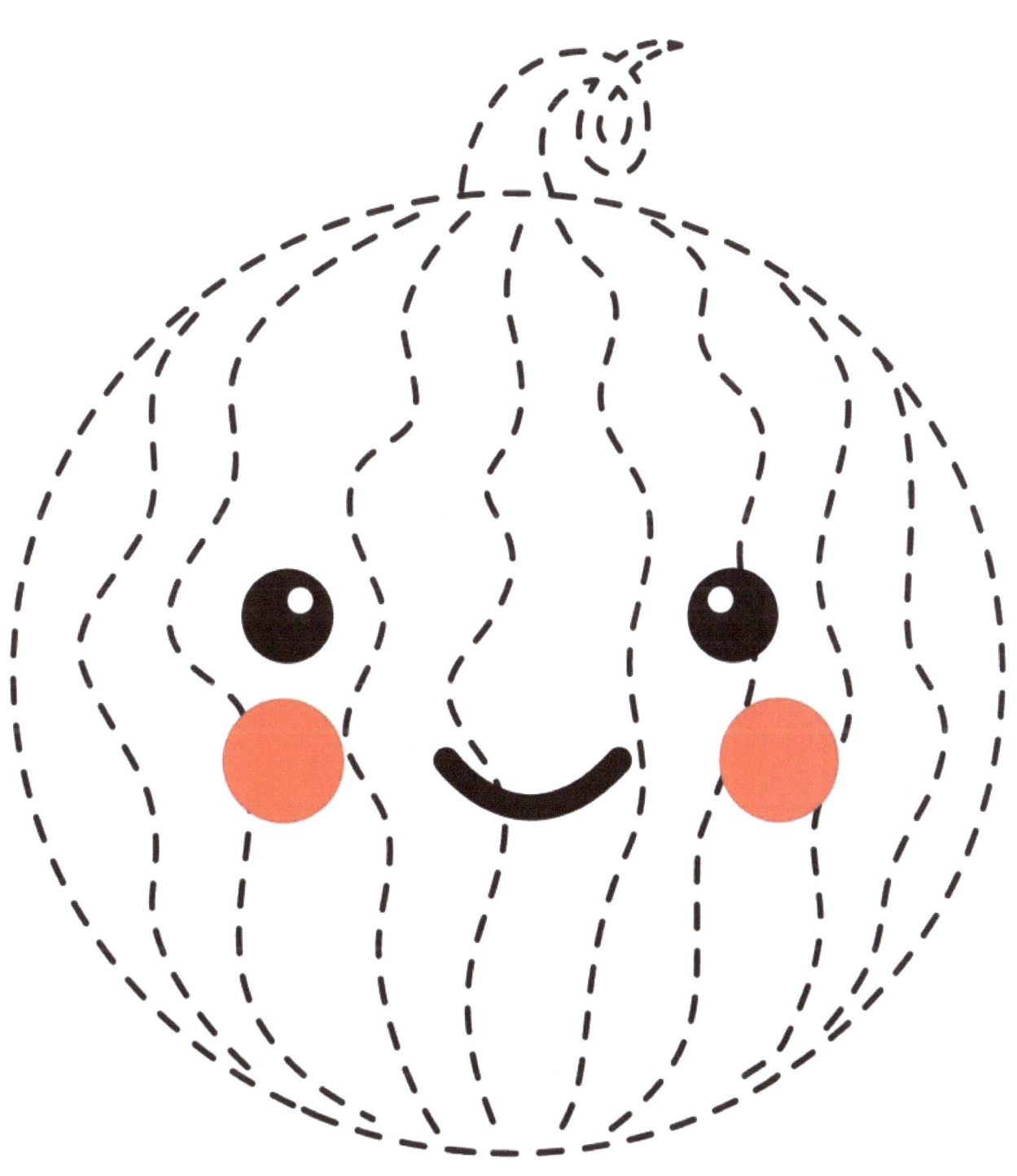

Whale Whale Whale

Whale Whale Whale

Whale Whale Whale

Whale Whale Whale

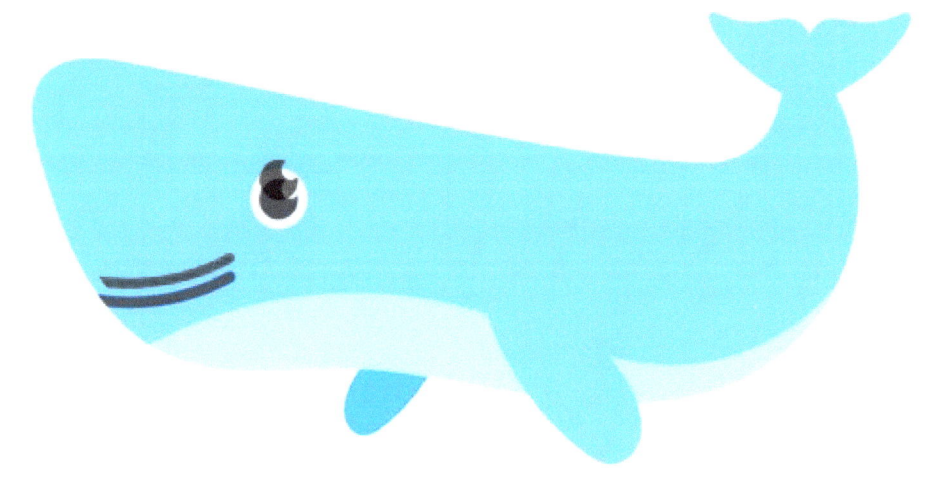

Whale

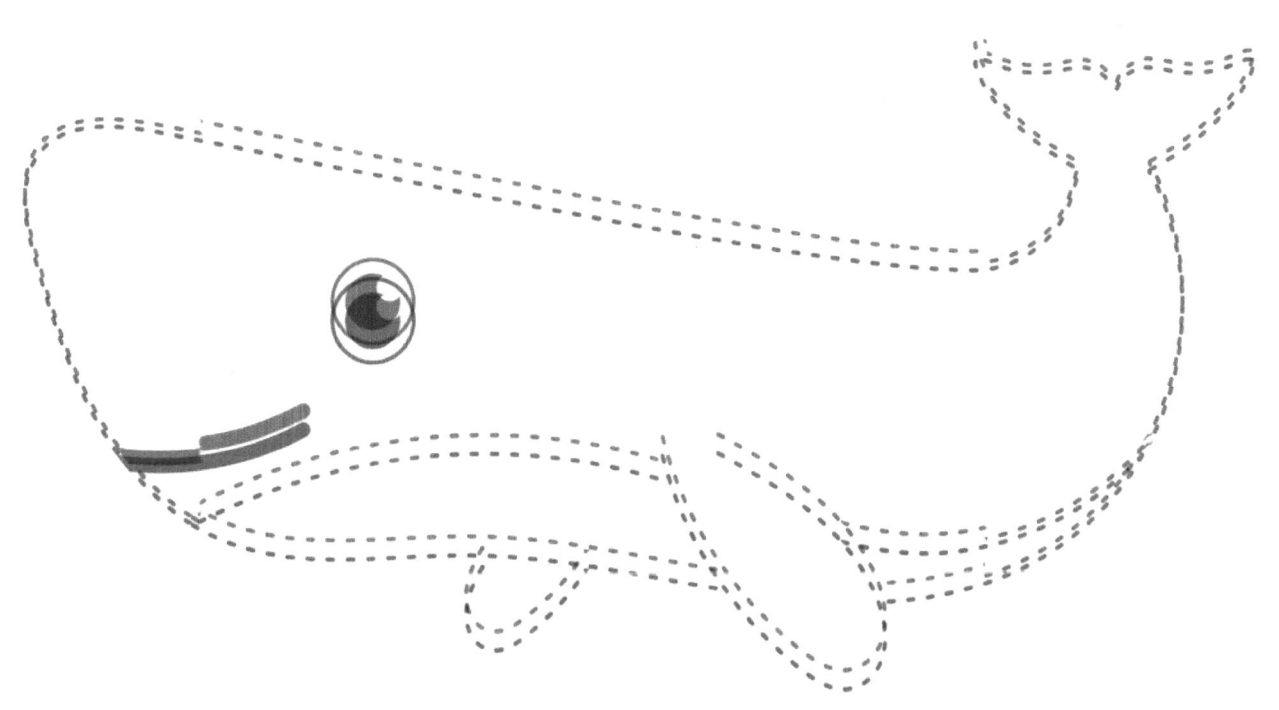

Xylophone   Xylophone

Xylophone   Xylophone

Xylophone   Xylophone

Xylophone   Xylophone

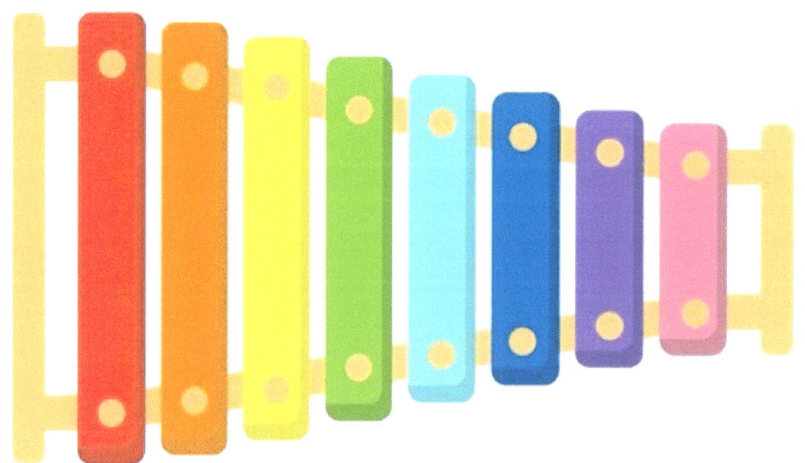

Xylophone

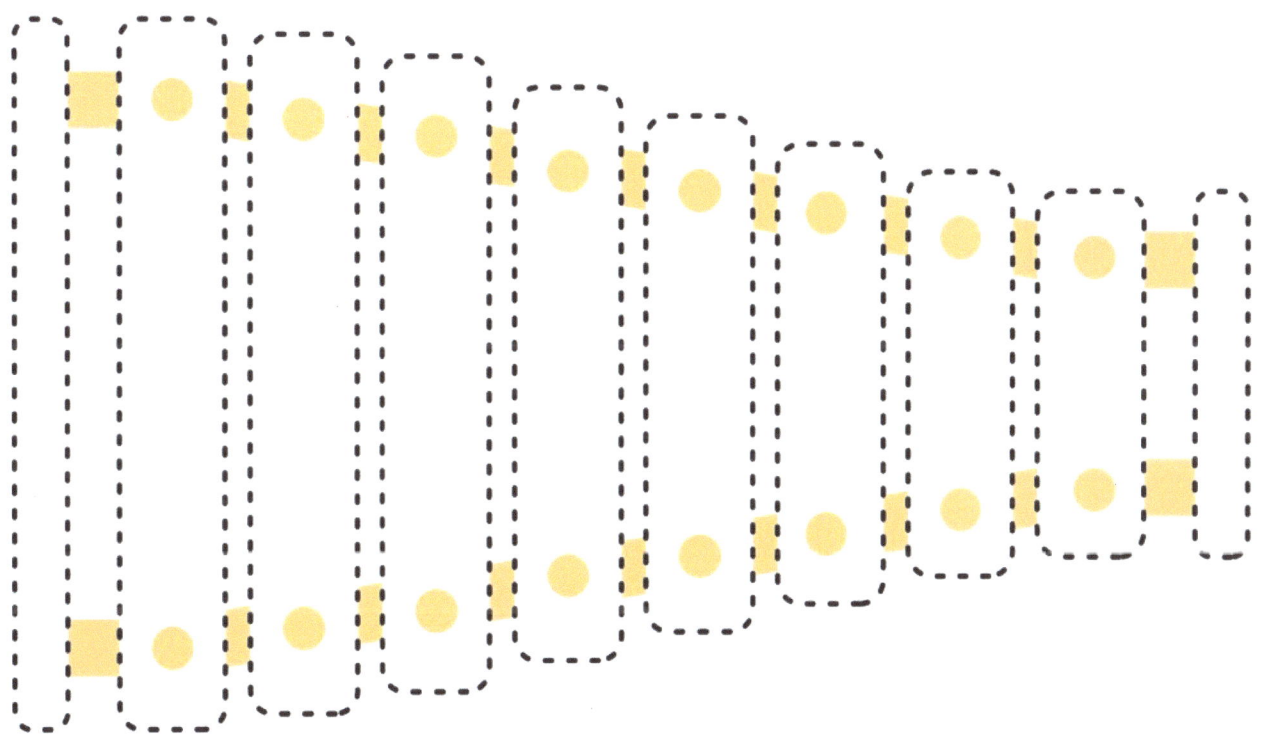

Trace & Color

BOOK 3